THE SIGNING OF THE
MAGNA CARTA

DEBBIE LEVY

TWENTY-FIRST CENTURY BOOKS
MINNEAPOLIS

Consultant: David M. Perry, Assistant Professor of History, Dominican University, Chicago, Illinois

The author gratefully acknowledges:
The British Library, for permission to reprint excerpts from the library's English translation of the Magna Carta. http://www.bl.uk.

Simon & Schuster, for permission to use excerpts from *1215: The Year of Magna Carta*, by Danny Danziger and John Gillingham. Copyright © 2003 by Danny Danziger and John Gillingham. Reprinted with the permission of Simon and Schuster Adult Publishing Group.

Primary source material in this text is printed over an antique-paper texture.

The photo on the cover is of one of four remaining copies of the Magna Carta that were sealed and sent out in June 1215. It is held in the British Library, London, Great Britain.

Twenty-First Century Books
A division of Lerner Publishing Group, Inc.
241 First Avenue North
Minneapolis, MN 55401

Website address: www.lernerbooks.com

Library of Congress Cataloging-in-Publication Data

Levy, Debbie.
    The Signing of the Magna Carta / by Debbie Levy.
        p.   cm. — (Pivotal moments in history)
    Includes bibliographical references and index.
    ISBN-13: 978–0–8225–5917–7 (lib. bdg. : alk. paper)
    1. Magna Carta 2. Constitutional history—Great Britain. I. Title
JN147.L48 2008
942.03'3—dc22   2005020971

Manufactured in the United States of America
1 2 3 4 5 6 – DP – 13 12 11 10 09 08

CONTENTS

CHAPTER ONE
THE MAGNA CARTA

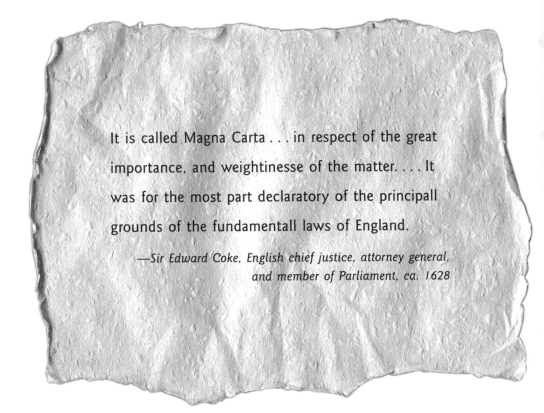

It is called Magna Carta . . . in respect of the great importance, and weightinesse of the matter. . . . It was for the most part declaratory of the principall grounds of the fundamentall laws of England.

—Sir Edward Coke, English chief justice, attorney general, and member of Parliament, ca. 1628

Question: What did a thirteenth-century conflict between rich and powerful noblemen and King John of England have to do with the rights of ordinary people?

Answer: Nothing.

Question: What did the treaty of 1215 that settled the conflict between King John and his nobles (for about three months) have to do with the rights of ordinary people?

Answer: Nothing.

Question: According to lawyers and judges, what document stands for the idea that ordinary people have certain rights, including rights to fair treatment by their governments?

Answer: The treaty of 1215 between King John and his nobles—namely, the Magna Carta.

Magna Carta: The words are Latin for "Great Charter." It was drawn up in 1215 between King John of England and a group of English barons and other noblemen who would have liked to see John thrown off his throne. King John's followers and the barons' followers had been fighting for years. Some of the less hotheaded among them thought that things might be smoothed over if the king agreed to a list of specific actions and behaviors that he would follow in his future dealings with his barons. That list was the Magna Carta.

A LIFE OF ITS OWN

The list was crammed with details about the two issues that most concerned the barons—money and property. The Magna Carta was about relations between the king and the great landholders of the day, a small group of barons who controlled pieces of territory that they treated as mini-kingdoms. Nothing in the list concerned the vast majority of the people in England. Most people—who lived in the countryside working on land that was not their own—did not have direct dealings with the king. These people, the peasants, mostly dealt with the barons and other nobles to whom they owed their livelihoods. And there was no Great Charter or even a small charter between nobles and peasants.

Even limited as it was to matters between the barons and the king, the Magna Carta was a failure in its own time. Three months after King John affixed his royal seal to the Magna Carta, he and the barons were at war with each other again. A year later, a French prince invaded England and was crowned king by most of the barons.

So the Magna Carta appeared dead almost as soon as it was born. Appearances, however, can be deceiving. For the Magna Carta had staying power, which is more than can be said for certain other parties in the struggle of 1215. King John died shortly after the barons elevated the French prince to the throne. The barons soon lost their enthusiasm for their French prince and sent him packing back to France.

In contrast, the Magna Carta came back to life and even took on a life of its own. As years passed, people came to look upon the document as standing for the idea that government power should be limited and that citizens—all citizens—have rights and freedoms that their governments may not trample. Although never intended as a charter of individual rights or liberties, it became exactly that. In time, the Magna Carta was no longer a document about efforts by the barons of England to keep King John's hands off their property. It became a crucial step on the road toward constitutional government—toward government limited by the rights of citizens.

A 1297 version of the Magna Carta is on display in the National Archives Rotunda in Washington, D.C., as one of the Charters of Freedom. Many people see the Magna Carta (1215) as a first step toward the U.S. Constitution (1787).

CHAPTER TWO

THE PRICE OF POWER

He sent his men all over England into every shire
[county]. . . . Also he had a record made of . . . how
much everybody had who was occupying land in
England, in land or cattle, and how much money it
was worth.

—William the Conqueror's method of surveying the wealth he
acquired through his conquest of England in 1066 (as
described in the Anglo-Saxon Chronicle, an imprecise history
of England written by various authors during the ninth
through twelfth centuries)

The conflict between King John and his barons in the
early 1200s grew out of arguments about property. A
person's wealth was measured in land, castles, livestock, and
crops as well as money. But the question of who enjoyed
the benefits of all that property could be complicated.

Ideas and customs about who owned what in King
John's England had roots in the actions of his ancestor,
William I of Normandy. Normandy was a large region in

the territory that is part of present-day northern France. In 1066 William and his Norman armies sailed from northern France to England and defeated the previous rulers and inhabitants of England, the Anglo-Saxons. England became a fairly small part of a large European empire centered in Normandy and ruled by William I— also known as William the Conqueror.

Although he took over England by force, William also claimed that he had a legal right to the country. He said that the previous king of England, Edward the Confessor, bequeathed, or gave, the kingdom to him when he died.

This eleventh-century silver coin bears the portrait of William the Conqueror.

England and France
at the Turn of the
Thirteenth Century

SCOTLAND

Berwick

NORTH SEA

IRELAND

York

ENGLAND

Oxford
Northampton
WELSH
STATES
R. Thames
Brackley
London
Canterbury
Gloucester
Sandwich
Runnymede
Dover
Damme

R. Rhine

HOLY
ROMAN
EMPIRE

FLANDERS
Bouvines

English Channel

CHANNEL
ISLANDS
GUERNSEY
JERSEY

NORMANDY
Paris

R. Seine

ATLANTIC
OCEAN

BRITTANY
MAINE
FRANCE
Chinon
ANJOU
TOURAINE
R. Loire
Boulogne
Mirebeau
BERRI
Poitiers
POITOU
Angoulême
Chalus
AUVERGNE

*Bay of
Biscay*

AQUITAINE

AGENAIS

MEDITERRANEAN
SEA

Frontiers in 1180
Eastern limit of English
possessions in France, 1180
Lost by English in France
by 1200
Regional borders
▲ Battle   • City

Miles
0   50   100   150
0   100   200
Kilometers

Under this claim, Edward the Confessor owned England and bequeathed it to William I, just as a person might pass on a farm or herd of cattle.

William claimed ownership of all the land of England, but he knew he could not control it by himself. For help, he turned to the noblemen who had supported him in previous battles and conflicts. These men—who had titles such as barons, earls, and dukes—had proved their loyalty to the king in the past. In exchange for their loyalty, their taxes, and sometimes their knights (soldiers), the king granted the nobles large pieces of land.

NOBILITY, FOR A PRICE

The barons and other nobles held their land as a badge of a personal relationship with the king. This relationship was about status as well as landholding. Membership in the upper ranks of the nobility was quite select. At the end of William the Conqueror's reign in 1087, the king's family and the highest-ranked nobles (perhaps a dozen of them) controlled one-half the land in England. Around two hundred other nobles held the remaining half. This pattern continued into the 1100s and 1200s, under kings who succeeded to the throne after William's death.

The top nobles, however vast their landholdings, did not exactly own the land. They were tenants—renters. Their landlord was the king, and they were known as tenants-in-chief, because they held their land directly from the king. And although relationships between king and nobles were personal, they were also marked by rituals.

TIMBER! THE ROYAL FOREST, TAKE 1

Although the kings of England granted and sold great tracts of the countryside, they considered some land too wonderful to give away. This land was known as the royal forest. The forest included not only wooded areas—what people normally think of

This fourteenth-century English manuscript illustration shows King John hunting a stag in his royal forest.

as "forest"—but also all kinds of other lands, some of which were inhabited. Strict laws applied to the vast lands that the king labeled as forest. The laws prohibited anyone other than the king (and his guests) from hunting animals there, cutting wood, allowing cattle to eat the grass, or otherwise using forest resources. Not even the people who lived in the forest could use its resources without royal permission. This was rather inconvenient for farmers who lived there.

If the king wanted to add a piece of land to the forest, he simply had to "afforest" it, or declare that it was forest. Penalties for violations of the forest law were severe. As an anonymous observer wrote in the *Anglo-Saxon Chronicle* (a rough history of England compiled by various scribes from around 890 to the mid-1100s), in William the Conqueror's forest, "Whosoever killed hart [male red deer] or hind [female red deer] was to be blinded. He forbade hunting the harts and the boars. He loved stags [male deer] so very much, as though he were their father."

These rituals made it clear to the barons that although they were elite and powerful, someone was more elite and powerful than they.

The ceremony in which a noble pledged his loyalty to the king underscored who was in charge. The rite, called homage, had the noble kneel before the king, place his

FATHER FIGURE

When the nobles of medieval England placed their hands in the king's hands during the solemn homage ceremony (below, from a fifteenth-century English manuscript), they were pledging their pocketbooks and their loyalty. They were also placing their wives and children in the king's grasp as well. When a noble tenant-in-chief died, his minor children (generally, those under the age of twenty-one) came under the king's control. The king controlled whatever property the children might expect to receive as tenants when they reached the age of majority

hands in the king's hands, and swear to be faithful to him. The king granted the noble a parcel of land—or "seised" him of it. Included in the grant was the king's promise to protect the noble's right to hold the land, so long as the noble kept up his end of the bargain. That bargain included an open-ended commitment to provide

(twenty-one). The control the king had over such minor children was known as wardship. Wardship sometimes was for sale. A person who bought the right of wardship from the king was entitled to use the child's property for his own profit, at least until the child became an adult.

The widow of a noble tenant-in-chief also came under the king's control. The king had to approve of her remarriage, but approval came at a price. Frequently, the king married off a wealthy widow to a man who wished to acquire her property. Of course, the new husband paid the king a substantial sum for the privilege of marrying the widow. If a widowed woman wanted to marry someone of her own choice, she had to pay the king for that right (and the king could deny her request). If a widow wished to remain unmarried, she was likely to have to pay the king for that right too.

the king with aid and scutage when the king asked. "Aid" was money the nobles had to pay when the king felt he needed some extra financial assistance, besides normal taxes. Such a need might arise, for example, when the king married off a daughter and had to pay a dowry to the family of the daughter's husband-to-be. "Scutage," also

This fourteenth-century French manuscript illustration shows pages helping their knights prepare for battle. Nobles sometimes provided knights for the king as part of their scutage (military duty).

known as shield tax, was assistance in time of war. In William the Conqueror's time, nobles were expected to provide the king with knights—actual soldiers—on demand. This expectation changed in the 1100s, when monarchs accepted money instead of men. With money, these kings could hire their own soldiers for pay.

PILING ON DEBT

The death of a noble often gave the king the opportunity to extract even more money—from the noble's heirs. (Heirs are a person's surviving relatives, including children and wives. In medieval times, only male children were generally thought to have rights to property.) In exchange for a payment, which was called relief, the king permitted the heir to continue as a tenant and keep the land in the family. Of course, the usual taxes, aid, and scutage continued to apply.

Altogether, the amounts an heir owed the king were often so large that the heir could not pay them off all at once. He was forced to pledge the money to the king, promising to pay off the amounts over time. As a result, the heir constantly owed the king money. This position made many heirs, when they became landholders, even more subservient to the king than the usual homage-and-taxes arrangement. So long as the king did not need a large sum of money immediately, the king liked things this way. The more his nobles owed him, the more they needed to stay on his good side. And the more they needed to stay on his good side, the more power the king felt he held over them.

THE DOMESDAY BOOK

As the self-proclaimed lord and owner of all England, William the Conqueror wanted to know exactly how rich the land—and, therefore, he—was. Twenty years after the Norman Conquest, he sent his officials into the countryside to take a survey of all the property they could find.

To the conquered Anglo-Saxons, it was bad enough that William had wrested the land from them and distributed much of it among his Norman noble cronies. To have the kings' agents scour the countryside in 1085–1086 to count every last acre and barnyard animal added insult to injury. The native Anglo-Saxons nicknamed the entire enterprise Domesday, or Domesday Book. The title mocked the concept of Doomsday, the mythical last day of the

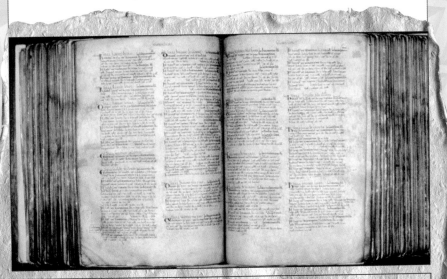

The Domesday Book is held at the Public Record Office in Kew, London, England.

This chest has held the Domesday Book since the beginning of the seventeenth century.

world, when everyone in the world will be judged and the results written down in a book.

In all, the kings' agents visited 13,418 places in England, taking note of the numbers of plows, mills, fishponds, people, and animals they found and how much the property was worth. The results of the survey were published in two detailed volumes. The Domesday Book survives to this day and provides a unique view of English life in the late 1100s.

PASS IT DOWN

Given their dependence on the king for their wealth, the top nobles in England developed resentments and grudges against the man who kept them from being truly masters of their own destiny. They were on constant call to fork over money to the king. Still, they were only too happy to impose the same system on others.

Like the king, the tenants-in-chief held so much land that they could not control it by themselves. Nor could they come up with the money they owed the king by themselves. So the highest nobles often gave other lords, such as knights, parcels of their land to hold as tenants. Knights often created subtenancies with other lords. Lords rented land to farmers who were not of noble rank. Of lowest status were peasants, who were neither landowners nor landholders at all. They merely worked and lived on other tenants' land. Generally, everyone who held land as a tenant paid fees and taxes to one lord or another, contributing to a complex web of economic and social relationships.

Peasants and farmers, with small amounts of property and wealth, did not like paying taxes any more than the tenants-in-chief did. When they had complaints, however, they usually had to take them to their lord and his officers. They posed little direct challenge to the person at the top of the social order, the king. In contrast, the tenants-in-chief's lord was the king. When they had complaints, the king heard them. And although the tenants-in-chief were dependent on the king, he needed them too. The king needed his nobles to make

A group of peasants have an audience with their lord before setting out to work in the fields in this nineteenth-century English woodcut of a fifteenth-century French manuscript illustration.

the land productive, so that they had money to pay him taxes and support him against his enemies.

Starting with William the Conqueror in 1066 and continuing through the time of King John in 1215, the kings of England aimed to strike a balance. They wanted to keep their royal treasuries filled with money. So they wanted to squeeze as much money as they could out of their nobles—without making the nobles so unhappy they would question their loyalty to the king. Put another way, the kings wanted to keep their nobles content but also subservient. This was not an easy balancing act.

THE FEUDAL NONSYSTEM

For many years, history books have described the medieval-era relationship among English kings, nobles, and common people as the feudal system. Under this concept, society was clearly divided into rigid social and economic classes. The classes interacted with one another in predictable, orderly ways. Many descriptions of feudalism suggested a strict hierarchy in which one class had authority over the class below it, which ruled the class below it, and so on, down to the peasants.

There were, indeed, different social and economic classes in medieval England. The king was the chief lord and landowner, and he did assert authority—with varying degrees of success— over lesser lords as well as commoners. But in recent years, historians have realized that relationships among kings, nobles, clergy, and ordinary people were more complex than portrayed in most history books. The people who lived at the time of the Magna Carta did not view themselves as part of a feudal system. Loyalties, fees, and other obligations did not always flow neatly from one social class to the class above it. People made arrangements to promote their well-being and protect their security, and sometimes this meant that their loyalties and obligations did not follow orderly patterns. Many historians have concluded that all this variety means that there was no identifiable feudal system—but rather, a complex set of social and economic relationships that resist easy categorization.

This drawing, based on a French image, shows the so-called feudal power structure during the Middle Ages. Notice how royals and the clergy are at the top, and peasants and knights are at the bottom. All of them are fighting, showing the power struggle between all groups.

CHAPTER THREE
DAILY LIVES

The only problems that plague London are the idiots who drink to excess and the frequency of fires.

To all this I should add that almost all the bishops, abbots, and lords of England are residents and, for all practical purposes, citizens of London. They have imposing houses there, where they stay and make lavish expenditures when summoned to the city by the king or archbishop to take part in councils or important gatherings, or when they come to deal with private business.

—William FitzStephen, a Londoner, writing around 1175

The customs in medieval England about who held land, and who owed what to whom, kept the vast majority of people—the peasants and farmers—indebted to the much smaller upper class. Ordinary people had to work hard to feed, clothe, and house themselves in a simple manner. For nobles, however, life offered rich possibilities and pleasures. They enjoyed plentiful food, sturdy homes, and the comforts of the times.

AT HOME IN A CASTLE

Wealthy people lived in manor houses or castles. These were generally built of stone and were part of huge estates sprawling over hundreds of acres of land. Manor houses included multiple buildings, such as a visitors' hall, a dining hall, chambers (bedrooms), and a kitchen. Manors even included indoor privies (bathrooms). The main buildings of a manor were often connected by covered walkways. Activities such as brewing ale and spinning wool took place in separate outbuildings. Outbuildings also included living quarters for servants and visitors and stables for horses.

Dover Castle in Dover, Kent, England, was built in the twelfth century. It is one of the largest castles in the country.

Although castles were the finest homes during medieval times, they did not exactly satisfy modern standards of comfort. Heated only by fireplaces, they were cold and drafty in winter. They were also dark and difficult to keep clean. Certain customs of the day added to the challenge of cleanliness. For example, although people were expected to use a privy when nature called, a manor's owner might urinate in his own visitors' hall. And although horses were usually kept outdoors, some manor owners liked to allow them in the main hall.

Meals were major events in upper-class homes. Many nobles skipped breakfast in favor of an early, hearty lunch. Servants regularly prepared lunches of four courses, with each course consisting of several dishes. Usually two to

BON APPETIT!

This weekly shopping list, drawn up by or for Eleanor of Brittany, a niece of King John, suggests that the rich in medieval England enjoyed quite a hearty diet:

Saturday: bread, ale, sole, almonds, butter, eggs

Sunday: mutton, pork, chicken and eggs

Monday: beef, pork, honey, vinegar

Tuesday: pork, eggs, egret

Wednesday: herring, conger, sole, eels, almonds and eggs

Thursday: pork, eggs, pepper, honey

Friday: conger, sole, eels, herring and almonds

ET HIC EPISCOPVS:CIBV:ET
POTV: BE NE DIC IT:

This detail of the Bayeux Tapestry shows William the Conqueror feasting with his barons. The Bayeux Tapestry was made in the eleventh century and is on permanent display in Bayeux, France.

four people shared a large dish of food, which was known as a mess. Each person had a platter with a thick slice of bread called a trencher on it. A diner placed a portion of meat or fish on the trencher and cut it with a knife. The trenchers absorbed juices from the food and were eaten along with it.

Lunch was the major meal of the day, but it was not the only one. Later in the afternoon, the lord and lady of the manor might entertain visitors for drinks. Around four o'clock, servants served supper in the main hall. It was lighter than lunch, with perhaps a single main course followed by dessert and cheese. Counting lunch, drinks, and supper, members of the nobility could spend five hours a day eating and drinking.

BIG BUSINESS

All that eating occupied many hours of the day, but the nobles found time for other pursuits. Lunch might be followed by outdoor entertainment, such as javelin throwing or heaving-the-stone contests. After supper, evening pastimes included backgammon, chess, music, storytelling, and dancing.

The illustration in this thirteenth-century French songbook shows women of nobility playing a ball game in a garden.

DRESSING UP, NOBLE-STYLE

In medieval England, the longer the clothes, the richer the person. Wealthy men and women wore leggings made of wool or silk. On their shirts, they favored very tight long sleeves. Some shirtsleeves were detachable and worn so tight that they had to be sewn on (by a servant) each time their owner changed clothes. Over the shirt, men wore long tunics and women wore long gowns with full skirts. On their feet, the wealthy wore thin-soled leather shoes that were not of much use in bad weather—but they looked good.

Of course, there were fashion trendsetters in the twelfth century just as there are in modern times. King Henry II found short clothes more practical than flowing outfits. For this fashion statement, he earned the nickname Henry Curtmantle (for short mantle, or coat).

But life was not all gluttony and games, even for the wealthy. After all, to stay wealthy, noblemen had to run productive manors that yielded rich harvests and large rents. A wealthy noble might hold twenty or more manors. Together with trusted assistants, the lord managed the affairs of all this property. At the top of the lord's to-do list was keeping track of his tenants. Some tenants, known as gentry, were quite wealthy themselves. A member of the gentry class—a status above common people but below nobility—might be rich enough to rent an entire manor and its lands. Other tenants held smaller pieces of land.

More complicated work was involved in managing land that the lord chose to work himself. The complications arose because the lord had to concern himself with operations of farmland, fishponds, and herds. He needed to ensure that barns and buildings were kept in good repair. He wanted to get the best prices for his farm's products, which could earn him more money than merely collecting rents. But the landholder could not do all this himself. Besides servants and laborers to do the physical work, he needed bailiffs and reeves to oversee the workers, clerks to keep up with paperwork, and treasurers to manage his money. In addition, he needed auditors to make sure his bailiffs, reeves, clerks, and treasurers were not cheating him. The lord also had to set up manorial

This fourteenth-century illustration from the Queen Mary Psalter (a collection of Psalms from the Bible and of prayers) shows peasants reaping under the supervision of a bailiff or reeve.

courts to resolve disagreements between his tenants and to enforce his powers over them. Running one or more manors was big business.

COUNTRY FOLK

While the nobility concerned themselves with the problems of administering vast estates, the vast majority of the three to five million people in England around 1200 lived on a smaller scale. They worked on small farms, holding the land as tenants. A farm of 10 to 30 acres (4 to 12 hectares) could support a family of five, producing enough food not only for eating but also for selling. The tenant farmer had to earn enough money to pay rent to the lord who held the land he farmed. He also had to pay taxes to the king and tithes (payments similar to taxes) to the local church.

Many country folk were not as well-off as the tenant farmers. They were villeins, or peasants who held land in villeinage. Villeins were not slaves, but they were not exactly free. These peasants were bound to their lord's land by law, exchanging their labor for a place to live. They could not leave and sometimes could not marry without permission from the lord on whose land they lived. Although villeins had no rights to the land, under long-standing custom, land held in villeinage usually passed down from generation to generation, much as did noble and tenant landholdings.

Ordinary farmers lived in small two-room houses made of timber. Roofs were made of thatch, floors of clay, and

ALE, THE MEDIEVAL HEALTH FOOD

Rich and poor people alike drank ale in medieval England. Most households made their own ale by mixing water and whatever grain was handy—usually barley but also wheat, oats, or millet. The mixture underwent fermentation, in which its sugars broke down into alcohol, and the alcohol killed harmful bacteria in the water.

Medieval ale did not resemble modern brews. The homemade ale was thick and sometimes even chewy with grain. Some people flavored it with spices, such as peppers. Only in the 1200s did brewers add dried hops (a type of plant) to the mixture instead of pepper and spices. This created a taste that modern drinkers are familiar with as beer.

walls of clay. Farmers grew grains, such as wheat, rye, barley, and oats. Close by the house, country people planted vegetable gardens. Most farms also had cattle and sheep for milk, cheese, leather, wool, and occasionally meat. Poultry, such as chickens, provided eggs and feathers—and occasionally meat. (Cows, sheep, and chickens that were kept alive provided food over long periods of time, while a slaughtered animal could only provide meat in the short term.) Some farmers were also beekeepers. Rounding out the farm family were horses and oxen, which were used to pull plows and carts.

Most country people ate lots of bread, which they baked themselves from stone-ground flour. They drank ale brewed from barley or other grains. Cheese and milk were also frequently on their tables, as well as whatever vegetables were in season. Eggs were generally a special-occasion food, and meat was eaten even more rarely.

In some areas, farmers' houses were spread far and wide across the larger estate owned by the lord. On other estates, farm families lived close together in a village, with their fields on the outskirts of the village. The lord of the manor decided whether he wished to establish a village for his tenant farmers or have them live in a more dispersed pattern.

ON THE TOWNS

Lords also established towns, or boroughs, in medieval England. It took plenty of money and effort to build a town. The founding lord usually had to build a castle for defense of the site and a church where the townspeople—called burgesses—could worship.

To encourage people to settle in their towns, lords promised certain freedoms to their burgesses. Burgesses were allowed to sell their town homes or pass them on to their heirs. They were also free from having to pay a toll, or fee, to attend the town's weekly market. Outside merchants had to pay a toll to come to the market to sell their goods.

Nobles and the king offered these freedoms and bore the expenses of creating towns, in the expectation that the towns would bring them increased riches. Townspeople paid rent to the lord to live in the town. The fee charged to outside merchants to attend the weekly market also went into the lord's pockets. Courts were established in towns to settle disputes between burgesses and to prosecute crimes. Court fees and fines added to the lord's treasury.

Towns offered ordinary people opportunities too. In towns, people could work as craftsmen, artisans, and

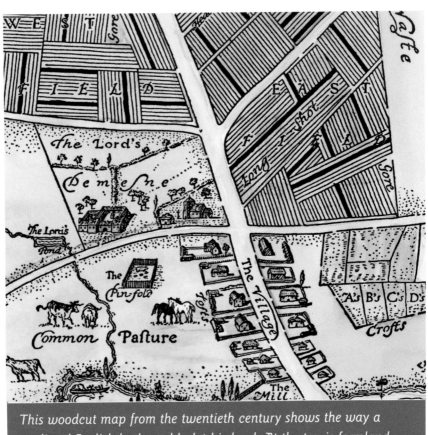

This woodcut map from the twentieth century shows the way a medieval English lord would plot his land. At the top is farmland, with the lord's manor home and the village below. Notice that the manor is at the center.

This illustration of a man shoeing a horse comes from a thirteenth-century British manuscript on the care of horses.

shopkeepers. Between 1066 and 1230, more than 125 towns were founded in England. Although the country was mostly a rural landscape, with very rich nobles controlling the land and lives of very poor peasants, towns allowed people to break out of the mold.

THE REACH OF RELIGION

One thing that nearly all English people shared in common—whether they were nobility or commoners, rich or poor, country folk or burgesses—was their church. Except for a few thousand Jewish people, the English were Christians, and their church was the Roman Catholic Church.

The Roman Catholic Church was centered in Rome and headed by the pope. The Catholic Church was very organized, with layers of officials in Rome and in countries such as England where the religion had taken hold. In England the top church officials were the archbishop of Canterbury and the archbishop of York. Below them were their bishops, and below them were thousands of other

This nineteenth-century hand-colored print shows the vestments (dress) of an archbishop (center), priest (right), and monk. The higher the official's position, the more elaborate was his clothing.

officials and clerks. Priests—clergymen who interacted with people on a daily basis, conducting baptisms, marriages, and funerals—were either vicars or rectors.

The officials of the Catholic Church were not rulers of the country. Still, the kings of England turned to the pope for his blessing over their rule. And although kings did not share power with the pope, they often sought approval of their actions from the pope or his archbishops. To have the church on one's side was a sign of moral authority and strength.

The church's influence reached deep into society. Its organizations and procedures operated much like a government. The church divided England into administrative units called parishes. Every parish had a church and a rector. The parish church usually held a large estate, thanks to a grant from the king or other important noble. The rector was entitled to collect tithes, money or crops equal to one-tenth of a person's farm output, from the population of the parish. The church also created its own courts to handle disputes involving clergymen and to decide questions involving wills and marriages.

CHURCH AND CONFLICT

Given that the church ran itself practically as a separate government, relationships among church officials, the king and his officers and nobles, and the ordinary people of England were sometimes difficult. Many people resented tithing and cheated on paying their tithes. Some working people chafed against church laws against performing labor on Sundays and religious holidays. They also resisted churchmen's lessons about living a moral life, which frequently included lectures about the evils of taverns—places that, for many people, were the center of their meager leisure life.

If interactions between the church and the general population resulted in a low-level hum of mild discord, relations among the church, king, and nobles could reach a much higher decibel level. The question of who was empowered to appoint church leaders was a major source of tension. For many years, kings and nobles took the

THE CRUSADES

In 1095 Pope Urban II urged the Christians of Europe to join in a holy war, or Crusade, to conquer the region that has come to be known as the Middle East. At the time, Muslims ruled much of that region's so-called Holy Land—the traditional setting of many events in the Bible. The pope and his supporters wished to drive Muslims out of the Holy Land and establish a Christian kingdom there. This first Crusade (1096–1099) was followed by others throughout the twelfth and thirteenth centuries. The Crusades attracted fervent fighters from across Europe. They aimed their violence not only at Muslims in the Holy Land, but at other non-Christians—Jews, in particular—wherever they were found. Some, but not all, of the kings of England supported the Crusades.

lead in appointing church officials. They felt it was their right to decide to whom they should give all the material rewards—land, buildings, and tithes—that went along with taking office as a bishop or other churchman. By the eleventh century, however, many church activists were arguing that the church should have more freedom from the king and other nobles.

By the 1100s, the kings of England were paying lip service to the church's arguments for greater independence and freedom. They said they agreed that church officials and monks (members of a monastery or cathedral who lived apart from the rest of society) should appoint their own bishops and other officers. Releasing the royal grip on church appointments was easier said than done, however. As it became less acceptable for kings simply to choose their favorites for high church positions, they turned to behind-the-scenes scheming and bribing to get their candidates in office. After all, kings had been used to getting their own way for centuries. It was not easy for them to let go of any of their absolute powers, whether their powers concerned their kingdom on Earth or the kingdom of God.

CHAPTER FOUR
THE KINGS OF ENGLAND

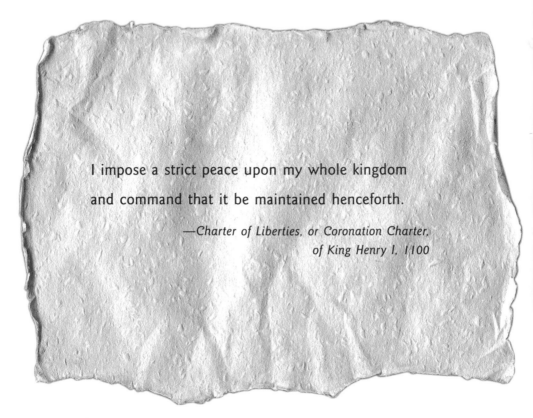

I impose a strict peace upon my whole kingdom
and command that it be maintained henceforth.

—*Charter of Liberties, or Coronation Charter,*
of King Henry I, 1100

The web of loyalties and landholdings that shaped
England's society and economy in the years leading up to
the Magna Carta also shaped the monarchy. The idea of
a nation was only beginning to take root. People thought
in terms of loyalty to a person rather than allegiance to a
nation. In a society where personal relations and power
were so intertwined, disputes over who was the most
powerful lord in the land were bound to get personal.

In fact, feuds within the royal family were common in the 1100s and 1200s. Members of the royal family often disputed who was entitled to claim the royal crown. Powerful nobles took sides in these disputes. Kings and would-be kings made promises of riches, power, and freedom to their supporters. Just as often, the royals squeezed their supporters for soldiers and money to shore up their efforts to hang on to or expand their empires.

HENRY TAKES CHARGE

The fighting over royal power began with the sons of William the Conqueror. Before his death in 1087, William put his oldest son, Robert, in charge of his original kingdom, Normandy. With Robert as Duke of Normandy, William tapped his middle son, William Rufus, as king of England (also known as King William II). Henry, the youngest son, received a gift of silver from his father but was not given a duchy or a kingdom.

None of the sons was content with his lot. Robert, William Rufus, and Henry spent much of their lives fighting (with assistance from their supporters) over the right to rule England, Normandy, and other territories in France. When William Rufus died in 1100, Henry moved quickly to claim the throne to England and became King Henry I (who ruled from 1100–1135). After a series of military expeditions, Henry also wrested Normandy away from his older brother, Robert, in 1106.

To help cement his hold on his kingdom, Henry issued a charter upon his coronation, or crowning, in 1100.

This document was intended to gain the favor of his barons and other nobles. "I take away all the bad customs by which the Kingdom of England was unjustly oppressed," he promised in the first clause of the charter. The barons could point to a whole range of "bad customs." William the Conqueror and William Rufus were both infamous for their never-ending demands for soldiers and other military support. People also resented them for imposing high penalties even for minor wrongdoings. William Rufus was disliked for demanding very large sums of money as relief, the payment required of an heir to claim his father's landholdings. William Rufus also extended the royal forest beyond the territory set aside by his father.

King Henry I's Coronation Charter, or Charter of Liberties, addressed many of the barons' complaints. For example, on the question of relief payments, the charter promised that Henry would take only a "just and lawful relief" from heirs seeking to obtain their fathers' land. The charter said that the king would not extract excessive penalties and that the forest would be limited to the acreage held by William the Conqueror.

Once King Henry got settled in his monarchy, he largely ignored the promises he made in his charter. Perhaps this was not surprising. After all, the practices to which the barons objected were part of what kept the royal family prosperous and powerful. Without more specific limits on royal power, the Coronation Charter practically invited King Henry I to continue to conduct business as usual.

KINGDOM OF CHAOS

King Henry I had a long reign but was no more successful than William the Conqueror in paving the way for a smooth transfer of power. His only male heir, a son named William, had died in a spectacular shipwreck in 1120, while returning from a successful military campaign with King Henry. Henry wanted his daughter Matilda to ascend to the throne, but the barons of England and Normandy objected to her ascension.

In late 1135, while on a hunting trip in Normandy, Henry was struck with a severe case of indigestion (some said he ate too many lampreys, a type of eel) and died. The question of who would be the next king of England and Normandy was unsettled. Into the uncertainty stepped Henry's nephew Stephen, with the backing of enough of the important nobles of England and Normandy to make his claim stick.

This fourteenth-century illustration from the Golden Book of St. Albans *shows Henry I's daughter Matilda holding a charter.*

Like King Henry I, King Stephen (who ruled from 1135–1154) issued a coronation charter in 1135 and followed it with a charter of liberties in 1136. Like Henry I, Stephen promised to follow only the good—and not the bad—customs and laws of his kingdom. And like King Henry I, King Stephen ruled as he wished. Still, the charters were not entirely without meaning. They showed that these kings felt they had to promise to exercise their powers fairly. The kings apparently did not feel that they could always do as they pleased with no explanation. The promises may have been hollow and not worth the parchment they were written on, but at least they existed.

King Stephen's reign was even less stable than the previous feud-riddled Norman reigns. Matilda (daughter of Henry I) continued to press her claim to the throne. In this, she was aided by her husband Geoffrey, Count of Anjou (a region in France), and his supporters. She also gained support among barons in England and Normandy. The kingdom roiled with war. Lured by money, land grants, and appointments to offices, barons switched their allegiance from Stephen to Matilda and then sometimes back again.

Chaos in the royal government enlarged the power and influence of the barons in two ways. First, they were able to wring promises and benefits from the competing Stephen and Matilda. And second, in the absence of a strong king, they exercised greater authority over their lands, the landholders, and the villagers under them. In courts that the barons created to hear the complaints of their villagers, a villager could rarely expect to win a claim against his baron.

After years of conflict, the royal combatants reached a settlement in 1153. King Stephen agreed to make Matilda and Geoffrey's son, Henry, his heir. And so in 1154 when Stephen died, King Henry II became ruler of England and Normandy at the age of twenty-one. Thanks to his marriage to Eleanor of Aquitaine, he also ruled that large French territory and another region of France called Poitou. Together these two areas occupied about one-third of modern France. Although Henry had promised Anjou to his brother, he decided to keep this part of his kingdom for himself. He also held on to Maine and Touraine.

Henry II used this red wax seal with his image to seal important documents.

THE KINGS OF ENGLAND, 1066–1216

From the region of France known as Normandy, came . . .

The Normans	Reign
William I, the Conqueror	1066–1087
William II, also known as William Rufus	1087–1100
Henry I	1100–1135
Stephen	1135–1154

After King Stephen, the line of descent switched to:

The Angevins (Angevin is derived from *Anjou*, as in Geoffrey of Anjou (a region in France), who was married to Matilda, daughter of King Henry I. Geoffrey and Matilda were the parents of the first king in the Angevin line, Henry II.)

Henry II	1154–1189
Richard I (the Lion Heart)	1189–1199
John	1199–1216

EMPIRE OF HENRY II

King Henry II's domains stretched from the border with Scotland in the north to the Pyrenees mountain range in France, in the south. (In legal theory, the English kings held their lands in France under the ownership of the French kings. Henry II, for example, was technically *King* of England and *Duke* of Normandy and Aquitaine. In reality, however, the English kings were independent of the French kings.) Henry II's holdings made him at least one of the most powerful kings in Europe, if not the most powerful. During his thirty-five-year reign, he also added Ireland to his domain. Henry II was very much a European monarch, spending more time in France than in England.

If he was going to rule over such a large empire, King Henry II needed to shore up the royal authority that had become eroded during the time of King Stephen. One of his main tools in repairing the kingship was the judicial system. He created new legal procedures by which villagers and tenants could bring property and other claims to the royal courts. He expanded the scope of the royal criminal courts as well.

King Henry II's changes brought more of the kingdom's law business into the king's courts rather than the manorial courts. This weakened the barons' hold over their villagers and tenants but strengthened the king's control over barons and commoners alike. Court fees (money charged for using the courts) and penalties (monetary punishments imposed by royal judges) began pouring into the king's coffers. Henry II also enlarged the royal forest by "afforesting" large tracts of land. He then tightened up enforcement of the forest laws, collecting large fines from people who infringed on the royal forest.

FAMILY FEUDS

Talented as he was in oiling the wheels of royal justice and administration, King Henry II could not smooth out

TIMBER, TAKE 2 (MORE ON THE ROYAL FOREST)

When William the Conqueror declared vast, rich regions of woodland and pasture as forest, he started a tradition that later kings embraced fully. By 1200 nearly one-third of England was considered forest. To lords and tenant farmers, the royal forest had become a royal pain. The king's foresters were everywhere, sniffing out forest offenses and barring people from using the very land they lived on. Lords and commoners were often united in one passion: their disgust with the laws of the forest.

squabbles in his own family. He and Eleanor had four sons and three daughters. The daughters, as was to be expected, married rich noblemen from foreign countries. The four sons spent their lives fighting over their father's empire.

Eleanor encouraged her three oldest sons—Henry, Richard, and Geoffrey—to rebel against Henry II in 1173. (John, the fourth son, was five years old, too young to be involved at first. The others were teenagers.) Eleanor's involvement probably reflected her own thirst for greater power, in Aquitaine and in England. It may also have reflected marital discord between her and Herny II. Whatever the reason, the rebellion touched off years of conflict. War spread beyond family members to involve nobles from England and Normandy, the kings of France and Scotland, and various counts in Europe. The costs of constant warfare required Henry II to press his barons ceaselessly for money and to seek larger and larger fines for breaches of the forest law.

Only death, it seemed, could calm the conflicts among Henry II's sons. First, the oldest son, Henry, got sick and died in 1183. Next, Geoffrey died in 1186. Richard was next in line as the king's heir, but Henry II refused to recognize this. Instead, he championed the youngest son, John, whom he had always favored. In response, Richard allied himself with King Philip Augustus of France and continued fighting his father.

This fourteenth-century French illustration shows Henry II laying siege to one of Philip Augustus's castles in 1189.

These tomb effigies from the thirteenth century depict King Henry II (left) and his wife, Eleanor of Aquitaine. Their four sons spent much of their time squabbling over Henry II's kingdom.

51

Finally, in 1189, King Henry II gave up. He had lost battles and lost the support of nobles throughout his French domains. Even John turned on him, probably seeing that his position was hopeless. Henry II agreed that his son Richard would succeed him to the throne as the leader of all his lands.

THE WARRIOR KING

On July 6, 1189, Henry II died. As soon as King Richard I (who reigned from 1189–1199) ascended the throne, he began planning the career that truly inspired him—that

This bronze copy of a nineteenth-century statue by Carlo Marochetti is of King Richard I. It stands outside of the Houses of Parliament in London, England.

of a crusader. Unlike previous kings of England, he was not satisfied with supporting the Crusades with money and material support. He was a warrior, and he felt the need to fight personally.

A year after he became king, Richard I set out for the Middle East. He was accompanied by King Philip

Augustus of France (who reigned from 1179–1223). In 1190 they captured an important fortress at Acre (in present-day Israel). The following year, Philip Augustus returned to France, but Richard continued to do battle. He and his soldiers failed to wrest Jerusalem out of Muslim hands, but they gained land in Palestine and negotiated a treaty with the Muslim leader, Saladin. People who witnessed Richard's warrior exploits on his Crusade gave him his nickname, *Coeur de Lion*—which is French for "Lion Heart."

While King Richard I was off crusading, he left his top ministers in charge of his domains. To these trusted ministers fell the thankless task of raising funds to support Richard's military campaigns. They assessed high taxes. They collected large fines for violations of the forest laws. They sold off titles and positions, taking cash in exchange for sheriffs' offices and lordships. They sold towns, castles, and pieces of the forest.

This detail shows two twelfth-century crusaders. The original fresco, a type of wall painting, is found in the Templar Chapel in Cressac, France.

FACT, FICTION, ROBIN HOOD, AND THE EVIL PRINCE JOHN

Children around the world have heard or read stories of Robin Hood *(pictured opposite page, in a seventeenth-century woodcut)*, the good-hearted outlaw of medieval England who stole from the rich and gave to the poor. One of Robin's defining traits was a strong disrespect for the king's forest law. As an early ballad, called "A Gest of Robyn Hode," put it, he

> always slewe the kyng's dere
> And welt them at his wyll.

Translated into modern English, these lines mean that he always killed (or slew) the king's deer and did as he pleased with them—which was to eat them.

The earliest ballads that refer to Robin Hood date from sometime around the 1400s. Those stories mentioned a king

BROTHERLY COMPETITION

Missing from this group of trusted nobles was King Richard's brother John. When Richard became king, he made John a count and gave his younger brother several counties in England and a county in Normandy. But King Richard did not grant John any real governing powers. This was not an oversight. After all the years of family but did not identify the king. As time passed, stories about Robin Hood multiplied and mutated. The stories that are most familiar to modern readers put Robin in the era of King Richard I (the late 1100s). According to these stories, Robin Hood protected Richard's authority when he was off on crusade and resisted efforts by the evil Prince John (Richard's brother) to steal the throne. No one knows, however, whether there was a real person behind the Robin Hood legends.

feuds, Richard did not trust John. In fact, at first Richard banned his brother from living in England while Richard was on crusade. But at the urging of their mother, Eleanor, he changed his mind.

King Richard's doubts about John's trustworthiness proved well founded. In December 1192, while on his way home from the Crusades, Richard fell captive to

Leopold, Duke of Austria. Two months later, in February 1193, the duke sold King Richard to Emperor Henry VI (king of Germany and also of the larger Holy Roman Empire). The emperor was willing to release King Richard—for a price. Richard sent home instructions to his ministers to raise the money for this ransom.

While Richard sat in prison and his ministers scurried about trying to squeeze more cash out of the kingdom, John started working on a different plan. In January 1193, he and King Philip Augustus of France made a pact. Philip Augustus agreed to give John fortresses in western Normandy and to support John's rebellion against Richard. In exchange, John agreed to give Philip eastern Normandy when John became king. (This was the same King Philip Augustus with whom King Richard had linked arms and gone off to the Crusades. But that was then, and this was now.)

The plot moved forward. By January 1194, John was in control of key fortresses in Normandy, thanks to King Philip Augustus. John returned to England to advance his position there. But around the same time, King Richard's ministers were able to pay the 150,000 marks of silver—a huge amount for the time—demanded by the German emperor. Richard was released, and he returned to England in March 1194.

Upon Richard's release, John turned against King Philip Augustus and tried to win his Richard's trust. Whether John felt remorse for betraying King Richard or simply felt that King Philip Augustus could no longer help him is not clear. Perhaps John had second thoughts about the wisdom of breaking up the huge empire put together by his father, King Henry II. Or maybe he simply had second thoughts about his ability to carry it off.

King Richard forgave John. The king, who never really put roots down in England, went back to France in May 1194. He did not return to England. (Richard spent less than one year of his ten-year reign there.) He was done crusading, but he was not done fighting. King Richard spent the last five years of his reign battling King Philip Augustus's attacks on his holdings in France.

In 1199, during a minor skirmish at a castle in Chalus, in south-central France, King Richard was shot with a crossbow. The wound turned gangrenous. King Richard died on April 6, 1199. He had been married, but he and his queen had no children to take over the kingship.

King Henry II, dead for a decade, finally got his wish. The baby of the family, John, was heir to the throne.

CHAPTER FIVE
THE TROUBLES OF KING JOHN

I do defy thee, France.

Arthur of Britaine, yield thee to my hand;

And out of my dear love I'll give thee more

Than e'er the coward hand of France can win,

Submit thee, boy.

—The character of King John, to Arthur of Brittany,
trying to talk Arthur out of rebellion, in William
Shakespeare's play The Life and Death of King John

In a ceremony at Westminster, England, on May 27, 1199, the archbishop of Canterbury, Hubert Walter, poured special anointing oil on John's head, hands, and chest, and declared him the new king. With this seal of approval from the church, John finally took the throne he had earlier tried to steal from his brother.

King John quickly found that his throne was not a very comfortable seat. King Richard I had repeatedly dug deep into the pockets of the population. He and his ministers extracted extraordinary amounts to raise Richard's ransom money in 1193 and then to do battle against Philip Augustus in France. King Richard's service in the Crusades and obvious physical courage earned him widespread admiration, however, even as he helped himself to his subjects' money. King John had built up no similar feelings of goodwill. With his reputation for treachery against King Richard, he would not have won any popularity contests. From his brother, King John inherited a kingdom under siege in its French territories, and in constant need for money. What he did not inherit was popularity.

So King John began his reign in some trouble. Things got worse immediately.

Trouble came at once from a challenger to King John's throne. Arthur of Brittany, a nephew of King Richard, claimed that he was the rightful king. His claim was not ridiculous. As the son of Richard's older brother, Geoffrey, Arthur was in the line of royal inheritance. Some years earlier, reacting to John's treachery, King Richard had favored Arthur to be his heir. However, by the time of King Richard's death, he had come around to recognizing John as his rightful successor.

Still, Arthur's claim attracted powerful supporters, especially in the French territories. The would-be king was only twelve years old, but his supporters were perfectly happy to help him rule through his teenage years. The province of Anjou was the base of Arthur's support. There, barons pronounced Arthur their new

This is the royal seal of King Philip Augustus of France. The inscription, written in Latin, translates to "Philip, by Grace of God, King of France."

monarch. King Philip Augustus of France took advantage of John's weakness and Arthur's potential by invading nearby Normandy.

At first, King Richard's popularity rubbed off on John. Honoring Richard's wishes, the barons of Normandy and England stayed loyal to King John. Other important leaders also declared their support for him, including Richard's allies in Germany, Flanders (part of modern Belgium), and Boulogne (in France). King John did not seem to inspire much loyalty or love, however, and his supporters wavered in their steadfastness.

FACE-OFF IN FRANCE

King John's troubles were just beginning. In August 1200, he married Isabella of Angouleme (a region in modern-day France). This match mightily offended one Hugh de Lusignan, who had been planning to marry the young girl (she was twelve to fifteen years old) himself. Lusignan was a powerful lord in Poitou, one of John's French dominions. The Lusignan family complained to King Philip Augustus of France about the damage John had done to their honor by taking up with Isabella, and to their resources by taking away the territory of Angouleme.

King John married Isabella of Angouleme (above) in 1200.

The king of France swung into action. He demanded that King John appear before him to explain himself. This summons was based in the French king's formal status as the head of all lands in France, with everyone, from William the Conqueror on down, holding French territory under his authority. None of King John's predecessors had taken this formal relationship seriously. Neither did John. He ignored the French king's demand.

In the face of King John's refusal to answer the summons, King Philip Augustus declared in April 1202 that all of John's lands in France were forfeited. He further declared that large chunks of these holdings—Poitou, Anjou, Maine, and Touraine—were transferred to Arthur of Brittany, who had earlier lost out in his effort to take over John's throne. King John, who was already in his French territories, responded decisively. He and an army marched to Mirebeau, in Poitou. There they took as prisoners Arthur and more than two hundred barons and knights. By this time, King John had the support of Anjou's most powerful barons. By August 1, 1202, he had successfully defended his empire in this latest struggle with the French king.

EMPIRE IN TATTERS

It did not take long for John to squander his success. He treated the nobles he had taken as prisoners in Poitou poorly. Twenty-two of them reportedly died of starvation while imprisoned under John's authority. The barons of Anjou developed second thoughts about throwing their lot in with a king who treated other nobles so cruelly. The Anjou nobles turned against King John, forcing him out of the region in January 1203. King Philip Augustus and his army moved in where John moved out, immediately taking over Anjou, Maine, and Touraine.

Meanwhile, King John's nephew and challenger, Arthur of Brittany, was murdered. Although no one ever discovered exactly who killed the young man, people

This nineteenth-century painting by W. F. Yeames shows young Arthur of Brittany with a monk. The sympathetic portrait is probably due to the widely held belief that King John had Arthur killed.

suspected that John had ordered the murder or had even carried it out himself. Either way, the killing of a kinsman being held prisoner violated all notions of decency. King John's reputation was completely spoiled.

If John had any chance of holding onto Normandy, the rumors circulating about his role in Arthur's death crushed that chance. Having lost the support of the nobles in Normandy and elsewhere in his French possessions, he had to rely on paid soldiers with no particular loyalty to him. Their military support was not enough. King John himself seemed to have lost the will to defend his claim to Normandy. In December 1203, he pulled out, sailing across the English Channel to return to England. The lords of Normandy, Poitou, and Aquitaine gladly submitted to rule by King Philip Augustus. By March 1204, John's remaining soldiers still fighting in France were defeated.

And so the empire of William the Conqueror, which had been defended and extended by John's father, Henry II, was in tatters. Of the French lands controlled by his ancestors, all that King John managed to hold onto were the Channel Islands—a group of nine islands off the northwestern coast of France—and a small region in southwest France known as Gascony. He was truly only King John of England.

PIECES OF ENGLAND

The Channel Islands are the only part of the French lands held by the Norman and Angevin kings that are still administered by Great Britain. (Great Britain is the name of the modern nation that includes England, Scotland, Wales, and Northern Ireland.)

KING JOHN, ACCORDING TO SHAKESPEARE

The English playwright William Shakespeare (1564–1616) knew a good drama when he saw it, and King John's life was full of dramatic twists and turns. Shakespeare's play *The Life and Death of King John* (probably written in the 1590s) weaves Arthur's challenge to John, King Philip Augustus's threats against John, and the nobles' fickle loyalties into a complex story. The play is not really historically accurate, but it does convey the atmosphere of conflict and crisis that surrounded King John's reign. There is no mention of the Magna Carta.

This nineteenth-century engraving of William Shakespeare by Benjamin Holl is based on a seventeenth-century print by Arnold Houbraken.

One frequently quoted passage from the play is the following sad observation, made by Louis, the son of King Phillip Augustus:

> Life is as tedious as a twice-told tale,
> Vexing the dull ear of a drowsy man;
> And bitter shame hath spoil'd the sweet world's taste,
> That it yields nought but shame and bitterness.

MONEY TROUBLES

Things did not go smoothly for John in England either.
The English barons and other nobles were not impressed
with John's roller-coaster ride in France. He did not
inspire confidence as a leader. And John's adventures in
France did not help the kingdom's financial health,
which had already been harmed by King Richard's
adventures. By losing Normandy and his other French
territories, King John lost major sources of income. He
needed to build the royal treasury back up to a
comfortable level, and he wanted to prepare for a
military expedition to reconquer Normandy. The English
barons knew whom John would target to help make up
his money shortages—them.

King John followed his ancestors in pressing his
landholders for payments of various taxes. But John put
his own special spin on the usual fees. He charged
scutage more frequently than his predecessors. King
Henry II had imposed eight of these taxes for funding
military operations in thirty-four years. King John
imposed scutage eleven times in seventeen years, at ever-
increasing rates as he built up a war chest to fund his
return to France.

Similarly, King John escalated the traditional payments
of relief, by which heirs claimed their deceased fathers'
lands, to new levels. For example, he demanded 4,500
pounds (a type of English currency) from a nobleman
named Roger de Lacy to inherit his father's lands. This
sum was almost equal to half of the king's yearly take from
all the sheriffs in all the counties of England.

Hardly a person or institution was free from King John's pressure to build up the royal treasury. Sheriffs who were in charge of counties had to pay more and more to hold on to their positions, as did other officeholders. Court fees and fines increased to fatten King John's coffers. Widows who became wards of the king when their noble husbands died were pressed for payment when they wanted to remarry. Orphans who were wards of the king were a source of royal income when King John sold off his right to wardship to the highest bidder. Those who paid for such wardships exploited the orphans' inherited lands for their own benefit, until the children reached adulthood—by which time they might be lucky to have a shadow of their wealth remaining.

PRESSING FOR PAYMENTS

King John also changed the usual system in which previous monarchs had allowed nobles to pay off debts to the king over time. Previous kings did not mind allowing nobles to remain in debt to the royal treasury. The nobles paid off the amounts they owed little by little, all the while incurring new debts for the latest imposition of royal taxes. This system kept the king in a position of power over the nobles, even if it deprived the king of an immediate windfall of cash.

But King John wanted his money, and he wanted it immediately. He had no patience for payments over time. When nobles did not pay their debts on demand, King John resorted to harsh reprisals. No cash to pay the king?

The king took over the debtor's land. No land to hand over? The king threw the debtor in prison. Not even important nobles escaped this type of treatment. William de Braose, a prominent baron, did not make timely payments to the king for lands he held in Ireland and Wales. In 1209 King John forced William to give up his lands and castles and also to provide hostages to the king as human guarantees that William would pay his debt. William responded by staging an armed rebellion in 1210, which did not succeed.

King John must have been concerned that other unhappy barons might have more success, so he became a monarch on the move. John had more than fifty castles, hunting lodges, and other lands (twice as many as King Richard or Henry II). He traveled from one house to another, spending only a few days at each one.

RUMBLES OF REBELLION

By 1212 King John had amassed a huge fortune. Among other valuables, he had more than thirty million silver pennies. This may have amounted to half of the total coinage of England. He felt ready to plan his reconquest of Normandy. In preparation, King John used his silver to cement friendships among some of the nobles in Europe, particularly in Germany, Flanders, and Boulogne.

Friendships at home were harder to find. Talk of rebellion rumbled throughout the country. In 1212 a group of nobles plotted, unsuccessfully, to assassinate King John. When he learned of the plot, King John added

This silver penny (showing both the front and the back and enlarged to show detail) *dates from the early twelfth-century reign of Henry I.*

guardsmen armed with lethal crossbows—which could inflict such horrible wounds that many considered them barbaric—to his traveling household.

Meanwhile, King Philip Augustus of France was not sitting idle. Encouraged by rebellious English barons, Philip Augustus announced that he would invade England in the spring of 1213. In response, King John sent a fleet of ships across the English Channel to the port of Damme in Flanders, where the French fleet was anchored. The English ships destroyed hundreds of French ships. This gave King John some welcome good news and eliminated any immediate threat of French invasion.

KING JOHN VS. POPE INNOCENT III

For much of his reign, King John was engaged in a conflict of wills with Pope Innocent III, who led the Roman Catholic Church from 1198 to 1216. The argument between the two leaders started in July 1205, after the death of Archbishop of Canterbury Hubert Walter. John wanted to appoint the next archbishop. Instead, Innocent III chose his own candidate, Cardinal Stephen Langton. John complained that the pope's action infringed on royal authority.

The pope ignored John's complaint and consecrated Langton as archbishop of Canterbury. In response, the king moved from complaint to action. He refused to allow Langton to return to England after the new archbishop-elect traveled to Rome to receive the pope's blessing. John also took over church land and property in Canterbury. Innocent III reacted by placing an interdict, or prohibition, on England in 1208. Under the interdict, church officials in England could not hold Sunday services or bury people in church cemeteries. John then seized the property of churchmen in England. (He argued that since they were not doing their jobs, they were not entitled to their property and income.) The pope responded by excommunicating John in November 1209. Excommunication meant the king was kicked out of the church.

At first, the king did not seem to mind his status as a spiritual outcast. Indeed, he gained a material benefit by taking over church property. He even squeezed some extra income out of the situation when he let churchmen buy back the right to hold their lands.

By 1212, however, facing an assassination plot and preparations by France for an invasion of England, King John realized there were some things money could not buy. He needed the moral support of the church to face down his rebellious barons and the king of France. So in 1213, King John did an about-face. He accepted Stephen Langton as archbishop of Canterbury. He allowed churchmen to take back their estates and their offices. He paid back the church for all the monies he had diverted from its coffers. And in a public ceremony of submission to church authority, on May 15, 1213, King John formally resigned his lands to Pope Innocent III and received them back in exchange for an annual rent and a pledge of homage to the pope.

King John gained admittance back into the church. He gained Pope Innocent III's support against the French invasion threat. But while he gained church support, King John lost something else—the respect of the barons of England. Many of them attended the ceremony in which John submitted his lands to Innocent III. And the vision of the king signing his kingdom over to the pope snagged another string out of the cloak of royal power and honor that was unraveling around John.

This twentieth-century illustration shows two ships from the thirteenth century. King John's destruction of France's naval fleet at Damme in Flanders was an important victory.

BACK TO FRANCE

By the summer of 1213, King John was ready to go on the attack against France. In June 1213, he ordered his army to sail across the English Channel again, but his expedition was postponed for lack of support from some of his barons. These barons, known as the Northerners (many came from England's northern counties) said that their obligations to the king did not extend to military operations abroad. John mustered other soldiers and sailed to Poitou, in the southwest of France, in February 1214. At the same time, he sent an army of his allies to Flanders, in the northeast.

The king had some early successes in Poitou, but by the end of June 1214, he and his army were on the run from a French army under the command of Prince Louis, son of King Philip Augustus. In Flanders his allies fought a pitched battle against the rest of the French army under King Philip Augustus. At the town of Bouvines, Flanders, on July 27, 1214, the French won a decisive battle. King John was utterly defeated. Ten years after he first lost his French territories, he lost them for a second time.

CHAPTER SIX
REBELLION OF THE BARONS

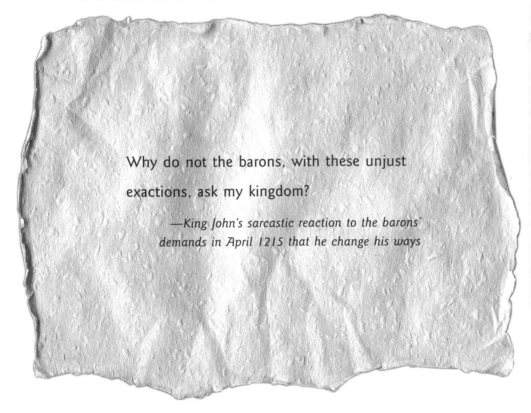

Why do not the barons, with these unjust

exactions, ask my kingdom?

—King John's sarcastic reaction to the barons'
demands in April 1215 that he change his ways

After the Battle of Bouvines, King John signed a truce with King Philip Augustus and headed home. Back in England in October 1214, his prospects were poor. His treasury was depleted by the costs of war. His reputation was deflated, both by his decisive military loss in France and by his surrender to Pope Innocent III. None of this made his restless barons, particularly those known as the Northerners, any more sympathetic to him. To them, he was still a greedy, power-hungry tyrant who interfered with their own abilities to amass wealth and power.

What was even worse, the barons saw John as a greedy, power-hungry failure. He had taken gobs and gobs of their money and still had not managed to hang on to the empire. That was what set apart King John from his brother, King Richard, and his father, King Henry II. They, too, had squeezed every penny they could out of their subjects. But they had successes to show for it.

LONGING FOR THE GOOD OLD DAYS

The disgruntled barons wasted no time communicating their dissatisfaction to King John. They did not demand anything too radical from him. To the contrary, they simply asked for a return to the good old days. Around Christmas 1214, the barons demanded that King John confirm the laws of King Edward the Confessor, from whom William the Conqueror claimed to inherit the throne. They also demanded that John embrace King Henry I's Coronation Charter.

This photograph is of a painting in Westminster Abbey, London, of Edward the Confessor.

A sort of hero worship had grown up around Edward the Confessor, as he was the king before the Norman Conquest in 1066 by William the Conqueror. People spoke of Edward as a reasonable and moderate king. King Henry I had made promises of reasonable government in his Coronation Charter. There was not much in the laws or policies of either Edward or Henry that could provide specific relief to the barons. Still, experience and custom were giving rise to the idea of an unwritten customary law of reasonable government.

King John still had some loyalists. Nobles who supported the king included William Marshal and Ranulf

ONE REBELLION AFTER ANOTHER

Every king of England since the Norman Conquest faced rebellions. English nobles rebelled against William the Conqueror because he conquered their country. Another generation of nobles rebelled against King William II (William Rufus) and then his brother King Henry I, insisting that a third brother (Robert) was entitled to be king. In King Stephen's time, rebels sought to unseat him from the throne in favor of Matilda, daughter of King Henry I. King Henry II faced rebellion from nobles who supported one or another of his rebelling sons. And King Richard I was opposed by John and the band of barons who backed his grab for the throne while Richard was held hostage after the Crusades.

de Blundeville. But those who opposed King John outnumbered his loyalists, especially in the northern and eastern regions of England. When John did not turn over a new and reasonable leaf by the beginning of 1215, some of these barons sent a formal written protest to Pope Innocent III. They complained particularly of John's recent demands for scutage to pay for his wars. King John sent his own representatives to meet with the pope in Rome. Despite John's years as an outcast, he presented himself as a faithful member of the church who asked only that other Christians obey him as good Christians were supposed to obey their king.

BACK TO BATTLE

King John knew he was not making progress with the barons when they came to a meeting with him in London in January 1215 with weapons at their sides. The barons said they would go to war against John if he did not confirm Henry I's Coronation Charter and make other changes. The two sides agreed to meet again in Northhampton on April 26, at which time the king promised to respond to the barons' demands. But those were just words. King John's real response was to prepare for war. He fortified his castles and hired foreign soldiers for pay. The barons, too, prepared for war, gathering supplies and allies and strengthening their own castles.

In Rome, Pope Innocent III was paying close attention to the problems in England. Church doctrine favored obedience to lawful leaders. Obedience, after all, helped

"King John, when he saw that he was deserted by almost all, so that out of his regal superabundance of followers he scarcely retained seven knights . . . deceitfully pretended to make peace for a time with the aforesaid barons, and sent William Marshal . . . and other trustworthy messengers, to them, and told them that, for the sake of peace, and for the exaltation and honour of the kingdom, he would willingly grant them the laws and liberties they required."

—Roger of Wendover, in his chronicle entitled Flowers of History (in Latin, Flores historiarum). Wendover lived and wrote in the time of the Magna Carta. He was not a fan of King John's.

church leaders manage their own extensive domains in many countries. Soon after hearing from both King John and the rebellious barons, Pope Innocent III announced his views on the matter. To be a just king, John had an obligation to hear the legitimate requests of his barons. That was the only good news the pope had for the rebellious barons. He said that alliances or unions that threatened war to try to force the king to do something were evil. Even worse, the pope directed the barons to pay the king's most recent assessments of scutage.

The pope's main representative in England, Archbishop Stephen Langton (whom King John had earlier spent so many years resisting), worked hard to find a compromise between John and the rebel barons. The king's loyalist, William Marshal, also tried to work out a settlement. But King John did not make their jobs easy. Riding the wave of the pope's support, he insisted that all nobles had to swear a new oath of loyalty to him. This demand was not particularly thoughtful or well timed. After all, the barons' disgust toward him did not disappear just because the pope said they should not be disgusted. John also earned the scorn of barons and others when, on March 4, 1215, he "took the cross" as a crusader. This meant he vowed to go on the Crusades to defend Christianity as his brother King Richard I had. This display of devotion may have pleased the pope, but many people saw it as meaningless show.

The barons showed up at Northampton on April 26, 1215, for their meeting with King John. The king did not. Nor did John send any communication indicating that he was even considering the barons' demands. On May 5, a group of the rebel barons met again at Brackley, north of Oxford. The pope may have disapproved, but the pope was in Rome. The barons formally renounced their loyalty to King John.

The barons' rejection of John was the equivalent of a declaration of war. Indeed, one of the rebel leaders, Robert FitzWalter, took the title Marshal of the Army of God and the Holy Church. But he and his followers did not have to fight anybody to take over the city of London on May 17, 1215. There, the people gladly accepted the rebel barons' leadership, as they had suffered extremely high taxes under King John. The ease with which London went against the king helped convince others elsewhere also to side with the rebels.

This charter of King John (above) was issued a few weeks before the Magna Carta, in May 1215. It has the same seal affixed that King John placed on the Magna Carta as a sign of agreement.

MAKING A LIST

King John appeared unmoved by his opponents' victory and showed no willingness to bend to the barons' demands for change. Behind the scenes, however, representatives from both sides met repeatedly. Exactly what the negotiators did, and when they did it, is mostly lost to history. But at some point in the first half of June 1215, they compiled a list of forty-nine demands. Around June 10, 1215, a group of rebel barons—decked out in their armor—met envoys of King John at Runnymede, a meadow on the Thames River. Again, no one knows exactly what happened there. The participants may have thrashed out the list in that meeting, or simply reviewed a final copy of the list, which contained agreements that had been reached in earlier meetings. In any event, this list became formalized in a document known as the Articles of the Barons.

In the following days, the parties modified the Articles of the Barons further. Again, the precise course of events is unknown, but a final draft of the document was produced by June 19. It bore the date June 15 "in the seventeenth year of our reign"—in other words, 1215— but the negotiators could have continued working out the details as late as June 19. King John went to Runnymede and affixed his royal seal to the document, indicating his agreement. This made it an official royal document, or charter. On June 19, most of the rebel barons renewed their pledges of loyalty to King John. War was averted. The crisis appeared to be over.

CHAPTER SEVEN
THE GREAT CHARTER

John, by the grace of God King of England, Lord of
Ireland, Duke of Normandy and Aquitaine, and Count of
Anjou, to his archbishops, bishops, abbots, earls, barons,
justices, foresters, sheriffs, stewards, servants and to all
his officials and loyal subjects, Greeting.

—*Preamble to the Magna Carta. Calling John "Duke of Normandy and
Aquitaine" and "Count of Anjou" was polite, but a stretch of the
imagination. By the time of the Magna Carta, John was only the king
of England and Ireland. His French authority was a thing of the past.*

The charter agreed to at Runnymede in 1215 (it was not
called the Magna Carta until later) was mostly a list of
practices that King John agreed to change. The king did
not agree to abolish his many privileges and powers as
the highest lord of the realm. Instead, he agreed to
weaken his royal rights in specific areas. In other words,
King John said what he had to say to quiet his rebelling
barons' complaints and avoid civil war.

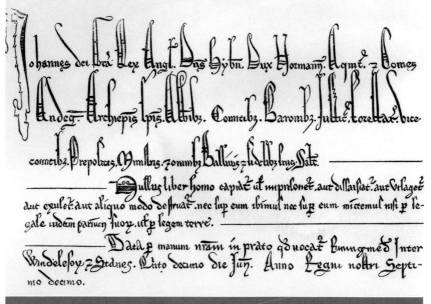

This engraving is based on one of the original copies of the Magna Carta held in the British Library. It shows the Preamble, Clause 46, and the Attestation.

In the charter's first clause, King John confirmed "that the English Church shall be free, and shall have its rights undiminished, and its liberties unimpaired." He pointed out that he had already granted the church the right to elect its own officials freely, without royal interference. The charter did not mention that King John came to grant this right to the church only after years of resisting it and years of disputes with the pope. The point was that the monarchy and the church now coexisted in harmony. And with that point made, the charter moved on to its nuts and bolts—royal practices. The main focus was fees and taxation, an area that the barons felt King John had abused.

THE PROBLEMS OF PAYMENTS

At the top of the list of these nuts and bolts was the king's treatment of a nobleman's property and family after his death. The charter addressed this subject in seven clauses immediately following the church clause. Clause 2 confirmed that a nobleman's adult heirs could succeed to his properties upon payment of relief. The charter described this as an "ancient" fee. By itself, that statement would not have satisfied the barons, as John and earlier kings had been extracting relief in ever-greater amounts for 150 years. But the clause went on to specify the maximum amounts of money that the king could require as relief payments (no more than one hundred pounds for an earl, for example). This specific type of limit was unprecedented.

Subsequent clauses addressed other situations that might be presented upon the death of a landholding nobleman. For example, if the nobleman's heirs were children when he died, the charter said that they would be entitled to obtain their father's land without having to pay a relief fee when they became adults (Clause 3). During the years that the children remained under age, with their property in the care of a guardian, that guardian was prohibited from depleting the land or other property to enrich himself (Clause 4). This clause was aimed at King John's practice of selling guardianships to unscrupulous people. As for a nobleman's widow, the charter promised that she should obtain her inheritance "at once and without trouble" (Clause 7). The king retained the right to approve a widow's remarriage, but he

LAND OF MANY TONGUES

England in the time of King John was a land of several languages. Some form of English was understood and spoken by most people. At the time, English was evolving from Old English to Middle English. Old English was based on the language of the early Germanic, Anglo-Saxon tribes that settled in England in the 400s.

The upper classes in England also spoke a type of French. This reflected the royal family's roots in Normandy and other parts of France. Poetry and other literature were written in French. Many French words also seeped into the English language, such as *baron, feast,* and *noble.*

Then there was Latin, the most highly regarded language of the early 1200s. People in the noble classes in England learned to read, write, and speak Latin. Latin was the language of the church, of historians, and of legal proceedings and documents. The Magna Carta was written in Latin, with many of the words abbreviated in the style of the time.

also agreed that "no widow shall be compelled to marry, so long as she wishes to remain without a husband" (Clause 8).

The nobles of England had as many complaints about scutage and its broader cousin, aid, as they did about relief payments. The charter took these up once it finished with relief. In contrast to some earlier practices, the king agreed that scutage and aid could only be imposed with the consent of "our kingdom." Getting the consent of "our kingdom" meant inviting the "archbishops, bishops, abbots, earls, and greater barons" to a meeting by sending them individual letters and having sheriffs summon the lesser nobles to this same meeting. This gathering of nobles before imposing a tax was not exactly a parliament or assembly, such as the kind democratic nations have in modern times—but it was an important new idea (Clauses 12 and 14).

CURING THE COURTS

With relief, scutage, and aid out of the way, the charter moved on to address another set of issues about which the barons held grievances. These concerned courts and the administration of justice. It was no secret that King John and other kings had used the justice system unjustly. In particular, they had used it as a means of wringing large fines out of the nobles. Thus, the charter provided that court fines would be more reasonable in the future: "For a trivial offence, a free man shall be fined only in proportion to the degree of his offence, and for a serious offence correspondingly, but not so heavily as to deprive him of his livelihood. . . . None of these fines shall be imposed except by the assessment on oath of reputable men of the neighbourhood" (Clause 20). The highest nobles also made sure that they would be treated with some respect in matters of judicial penalties: "Earls and barons shall be fined only by their equals, and in proportion to the gravity of their offence" (Clause 21).

It was also widely agreed that the king's sheriffs and constables (officials similar to modern police) tended to abuse their positions as the frontline enforcers of the king's laws and his courts' rulings. Accordingly, the charter offered several ways to rein them in. Clause 28 stated, "No constable or other royal official shall take corn or other movable goods from any man without immediate payment, unless the seller voluntarily offers postponement of this." This was an effort to prevent constables and others from using their powers of intimidation to pressure landholders into giving them crops and other goods. ("Corn" in Clause 28 referred to all types of grain.) Similarly, "No sheriff, royal official, or other person shall take horses or carts for transport from any free man, without his consent" (Clause 30). And "Neither we nor any royal officials will take wood for our castle, or for any other purpose, without the consent of the owner" (Clause 31). Besides these specific limitations, the charter put forth the commendable notion that the king's legal officials should know a thing or two about legal matters: "We will appoint as justices, constables, sheriffs, or other officials, only men that know the law of the realm and are minded to keep it well" (Clause 45).

When the machinery of justice was not being abused by the king or his officials, it could actually serve good purposes in settling property and other disputes in English society. This was reflected in Clause 18 of the charter, in which the king agreed to send his justices out into the countryside to hold court more frequently than they otherwise might have. Clause 17 also recognized the need for the regular hearing of legal disputes, providing that "ordinary lawsuits shall not follow the royal court around, but shall be held in a fixed place."

MATTERS OF FAIRNESS

In Clauses 39 and 40, the charter announced two sweeping principles of justice. The first principle barred the king or his agents from imprisoning, outlawing, or depriving "any free man" of his rights "except by the lawful judgement of his equals or by the law of the land" (Clause 39). The second principle promised that the king would not sell, deny, or delay justice (Clause 40). These broad principles were set forth without fanfare or explanation. Those who wrote them do not appear to have thought that they were saying anything remarkable. Certainly, by inserting these clauses in the middle of the charter, the authors indicated that they did not mean to give them any special significance. Yet of all the clauses in the charter, these principles struck a special chord with people who read them and heard them. These principles became the symbols of the Magna Carta.

Like other clauses in the charter, Clauses 39 and 40 probably reflected a mix of the authors' sense of what

England's custom already was and what they wanted England's custom to be. It was not a new idea, for example, that justice should not be for sale (Clause 39). Yet, under King John and other kings, there were many occasions when money, not the impartial application of law, bought favorable decisions in court. Nor was it a new idea that sheriffs should know and obey the laws that they were enforcing (Clause 45). When kings sold sheriff titles to the highest bidders, however, some sheriffs were bound to be lawless ignoramuses. It was also fairly obvious that punishment should fit the crime (Clause 20). However, when kings were allowed to use the legal system to extract money from people or to retaliate against enemies, this principle sometimes fell by the wayside. By writing down definitions of fair practices and limitations on royal authority, the Magna Carta took ideas of justice that most people accepted and made them something like enforceable law.

ODDS AND ENDS

Clauses on royal taxation and the justice system formed the heart of the Magna Carta. But there was more to the document. Several sections dealt with matters of concern to small groups of people. For example, Clauses 10 and 11 addressed debts people owed to England's Jewish moneylenders. (At the time, Jewish people, but not Christians, were allowed to engage in the business of money lending. Lending money for a fee was considered contrary to Christian practice. The Jews' success at this

This fourteenth-century English manuscript illustration shows a man beating three Jews, identified by the white patches on their clothes. Jews suffered persecution throughout Medieval Europe.

and other businesses led English Christians to come to resent and persecute them.) Clause 33 directed that fish-weirs (a type of net) should be removed from the Thames and other rivers in England, to improve navigation along those waterways. Under Clause 35, the king announced that standard weights and measurements should be established for wine, ale, corn, and cloth, which would help merchants and traders conduct business. Trade was also the subject of Clause 41, which provided that merchants could enter, travel in, and leave England "unharmed and without fear."

The charter addressed the hated forest laws, but only in a limited way. In Clause 47, King John vowed that "all forests that have been created in our reign shall at once be disafforested." As the greater expansion of the forest had taken place under King John's father, King Henry II, and not King John, this promise did not amount to much.

Some clauses aimed to erase specific problems in King John's relations with other nobles. These persons were mentioned by name. "We will at once return the sons of Llywelyn," John promised in Clause 58. Llywelyn was the leader of Wales. He made similar promises in Clause 59 about "the return of the sisters and hostages of Alexander, king of Scotland."

REINING IN THE KING

At the end of the charter, King John made one more announcement, and it was rather amazing. In Clause 61, he empowered the barons to elect a commission of twenty-five barons from among themselves. The commission's job was to "cause to be observed with all their might, the peace and liberties granted and confirmed to them by this charter." And when the charter said "with all their might," it seemed to mean it. This was to be no toothless committee but one with actual powers.

Any four of the barons elected to the commission could declare an act of the king or his officials contrary to the terms of the charter. If the king did not correct the problem, the four barons were to bring the matter to the full commission of twenty-five. By a majority vote, the commission could decide to seize the king's lands, castles, and possessions. The charter assumed that such an action would cause the king to remedy his evil ways. "Having secured the redress [correction of the violation]," Clause 61 noted, "they [the barons] may then resume their normal obedience to us."

The clause describing the commission of barons was the longest section of the Magna Carta. It took quite a lot of text to explain such a novel body—part legislature, part court, and part police department. Other sections of the charter gave the commission two additional and remarkable jobs. One was the duty to decide whether fines previously imposed by King John were unjust and therefore should be refunded (Clause 55). The other was the obligation to determine whether King John's previous seizure of lands or castles or deprivations of rights were unjust. If the barons found that the king had acted wrongly, they were empowered to restore the lands, castles, or rights to the person who had been deprived (Clause 52).

WHERE ARE THEY?

Four copies of the original Magna Carta dated June 15, 1215, are still in existence. Each looks a little different from the other, varying in size and shape. Each contains slight variations in text as well, but none is more official than another. Two are in the British Library in London, England, and the others are in the archives of Lincoln Cathedral and Salisbury Cathedral in Great Britain.

The Magna Carta memorial (above) stands at Runnymede. It was designed by Sir Edward Maufe and dedicated in 1957.

Under these clauses, then, the king was clearly subject to the rule of law. Law and justice were not simply what the king declared them to be but what a majority of elected officials decided, following the principles of the Magna Carta. The barons at Runnymede may have intended only to get King John off their backs and out of their pockets. But in reaching for this self-serving goal, they wrote a document that firmly supported the conclusion that the king was not above the law—and they got the king to agree to it.

CHAPTER EIGHT

THE FAILED CHARTER

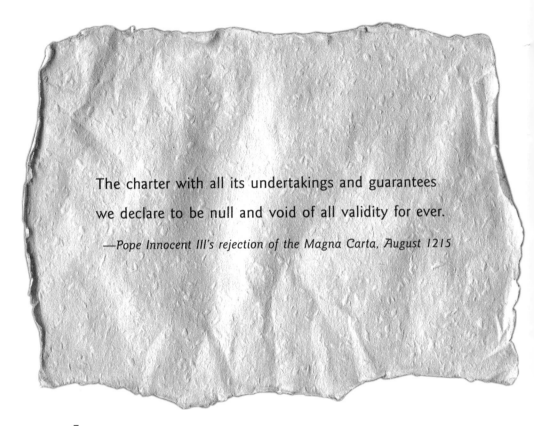

The charter with all its undertakings and guarantees
we declare to be null and void of all validity for ever.

—*Pope Innocent III's rejection of the Magna Carta, August 1215*

It was, perhaps, too much too soon. Perhaps it was too revolutionary to take root. After all, the charter authorized King John's opponents (the barons) to elect a commission made up of his opponents (twenty-five of those barons). That commission had the power to pass judgment over the king and even to take away the king's property. On top of that, the barons had threatened war to get King John to agree to the charter. Such arm-twisting was not just an insult—it was an attack on authority. King John did not like it, and he knew someone else who would share his distaste for the barons' disrespect of authority—the pope.

In the weeks following the agreement at Runnymede, King John went through the public motions of implementing the charter. Royal scribes penned copies of the document. The copies were sent out to sheriffs of the counties and bishops of the parishes, with instructions that they should hold public readings of the charter. The king issued another writ, or order, directing that elections should be held for the knights' committees that would investigate "evil customs" under Clause 48. At the same time, the barons selected their commission of twenty-five, which immediately began considering complaints filed against the king by other barons.

Privately, however, King John took steps to unwind the promises he had made at Runnymede. He enrolled paid foreign soldiers in the event he needed to take

INKING THE DEAL

Royal scribes wrote the charter on stretched sheepskin, known as vellum or parchment. They used long feather quill pens and ink made from oak tree galls (little bumps containing liquid). King John did not sign the charter. Instead, he followed the usual practice of the time, which was to affix to the copies of the document his great seal, made from beeswax and plant resins.

military action against his own barons. In July 1215, he
sent a secret letter to Pope Innocent III asking him to
declare the charter invalid. On August 24, 1215,
Innocent III issued his reply. It was an official document,
known as a papal bull. The bull reached England toward
the end of September. In it, the pope declared the charter
completely illegal.

*This papal bull (document) was issued in June 1216. The papal bull
issued by Pope Innocent III in August 1215 probably looked much like it.*

TWO THUMBS DOWN

Pope Innocent III did not mince words in his denunciation of the Magna Carta, which he issued in August 1215. The charter, he wrote, was:

... not only shameful and base but also illegal and unjust.... Since the whole crusade would be undermined if concessions of this sort were extorted from a great prince who had taken the cross, we, on behalf of Almighty God, Father, Son and Holy Ghost, and by the authority of Saints Peter and Paul His apostles, utterly reject and condemn this settlement. Under threat of excommunication we order that the king should not dare to observe and the barons and their associates should not insist on its being observed.

FROM BAD TO WORSE

While King John was laying the groundwork for throwing off the charter, the commission of twenty-five barons was busy ruling on claims against the king. Some of the barons' rulings were not controversial, such as the decision that Eustace de Vesci had a right to keep his dogs in the Northumberland forest. Others were serious slaps at the king's authority.

For example, the barons were quick to award Hertford castle to Robert FitzWalter, one of the king's most bitter enemies. They agreed with FitzWalter that the king had wrongfully taken Hertford away from him. When King

Alexander of Scotland pressed his claim to three counties on the border between England and Scotland, the barons ruled in his favor too. Nicholas de Stuteville complained that back in 1205, the king had accepted a huge sum of money as relief for Stuteville to obtain family lands. The amount was far too large for Stuteville to pay off, so instead he had given the king two manors as guarantees of his debt. Stuteville said that he was the victim of a raw deal. The barons agreed. At the end of September 1215, they told the royal official who held the manors that he must immediately give one of them back to Stuteville.

Then a bitter dispute arose between King John and Archbishop of Canterbury Stephen Langton. Langton controlled Rochester Castle, an important fortress located in southeastern England. The castle lay between London (in the country's interior) and royal military posts and ports around Kent (near the coast of the English Channel). If the king needed to bring in paid

Stephen Langton's seal (above) shows the archbishop in his vestments with his right hand raised in the benediction and his left hand holding a staff.

Rochester Castle still stands in Kent, England.

foreign soldiers from Europe, they would arrive at those posts in order to march toward London. On any such march, the soldiers would pass by Rochester Castle. Thus King John wanted it to be in loyal hands.

By August 1215, King John had decided that he wished to transfer the castle to a friendlier bishop, Peter des Roches. In the months leading up to the Magna Carta, Stephen Langton had walked a careful line between the king and the rebels, attempting to settle their disputes. But faced with John's demand, he chose sides. Langton refused to transfer the castle as the king demanded. Instead, in late September 1215, he fled England and had an ally give the castle to the barons. King John denounced Langton as "a notorious and barefaced traitor."

ANOTHER WAR

All pretense of cooperation between the barons and King John fell away. The war that had been suppressed at Runnymede broke out into the open. With his foreign soldiers imported from Europe, John marched from Dover on the coast toward London. Their route took them first to Rochester Castle, which the newly rebellious rebels had reinforced with their own soldiers. The rebels' soldiers shut themselves up in the castle, keeping King John and his forces at bay. In October 1215, the king and his men dug in for a long siege. They bombarded the castle walls with large stone-throwing weapons and chipped away at the castle walls with pickaxes.

By late November 1215, the king's men had broken down everything but the sturdy castle tower. While his soldiers hacked into the earth at the tower's base, King John sent off an order to one of his loyal officials: "Send to us with all speed by day and night forty of the fattest pigs of the sort least good for eating so that we can bring fire beneath the tower." The doomed pigs made their way to the king's camp. The soldiers built fires in the pits they had dug under the tower, and the king's nice, fat pigs (but not nice enough for eating) were used as fuel to keep the fires roaring. The tower collapsed, and its defenders surrendered on November 30, 1215.

During the siege of Rochester Castle, King John and the rebel barons both sent requests for assistance to King Philip Augustus of France and his son, Prince Louis. King Philip Augustus did not seem eager to get

English soldiers use a trebuchet (a large stone-throwing weapon) during a siege on a French city in this thirteenth-century French manuscript.

involved. Prince Louis, however, was game for adventure—especially when he learned what the rebel barons were willing to give him. They wanted no further negotiations with King John. They needed a person of royal blood to take over the monarchy. And so the barons offered the prince of France a whole new kingdom—England. It was not exactly a repeat of the Norman Conquest. But once again, a prince of France would come across the English Channel to claim the throne of England.

A FRENCH KING FOR ENGLAND

Prince Louis needed time to gather a French army to take to England. While he organized his forces, he sent a small group of French knights and soldiers (a few thousand men in all) to London. That city was a rebel stronghold, and the French reinforcements were meant to keep it that way. King John turned his attention to England's northern regions, where rebel barons also held power. Marching through the countryside, the king's troops defeated the rebel forces. King John even took the battle into Scotland, where King Alexander II supported the rebel barons. There, John captured the country's largest town, Berwick, in January 1216.

Despite his military victories, King John was not gaining support. To the contrary, his military methods turned many people against him. Because he was low on money and resources, King John encouraged his soldiers to ransack the towns and manors they defeated. As they tore through the northern counties and then headed for the eastern region of England, they helped themselves to food and livestock. They threatened to burn towns and villages to the ground unless the inhabitants paid money to the king.

Meanwhile, as King John stormed through the north and east, Prince Louis was on his way to England. The French prince landed in Sandwich, on the English coast, on May 22, 1216. Although King John had soldiers in the area, he did not fight the invasion. (Weather or concerns about the reliability of his soldiers may have played a part in his inaction.)

A KING'S CRUELTIES

Roger of Wendover lived during John's time and died in 1236. He wrote *Flowers of History* (in Latin, *Flores historiarum*), a not entirely reliable work that claimed to describe history from the biblical Creation up to 1235. As a fierce enemy of King John, Wendover put everything John did in the worst possible light. So the writer's account of John's harsh military methods in the northern and eastern countryside in early 1216 probably contains exaggerations. Still, even if the chronicle is only partly true, it paints an ugly picture and suggests why the king's military victories did not translate into true support of his rule:

These limbs of the devil [King John's soldiers] covered the whole country like locusts. Sword in hand they ransacked towns, houses, cemeteries, churches, robbing everyone, sparing neither women nor children. They put the king's enemies in chains until they paid a heavy ransom. Even priests at the altar were seized, tortured and robbed. Knights and others were hung up by their feet and legs or by their hands, fingers and thumbs, salt and vinegar were thrown into their eyes; others were roasted over burning coals and then dropped into cold water. None was released until they had handed over all the money they had to their torturers.

Instead, he went south to his residence in Winchester, allowing Prince Louis and his army to march to London. There, barons and other people of London greeted the prince enthusiastically. The rebel leader Robert FitzWalter swore allegiance to Louis as the new king of England. By June two-thirds of all English barons adopted Louis as their king, representing most of the eastern part of the country. King Alexander II of Scotland also traveled to England to pay homage to Louis and recognize him as the king of England.

FIGHTING TO THE END

King John avoided battle with Prince Louis or anyone else until September 1216. By this time, he had lost the support of many of his own household knights, who may have been disgusted by the king's failure to fight for his kingdom against the French invasion. However, King John knew that Louis and the French soldiers had been having problems of their own. The French had failed in an effort to conquer the town of Dover. Perhaps hoping to take advantage of Louis's difficulties, John finally went on the offensive in the northeast of England. John defeated the rebels' supporters in Lincoln and moved southeast to Lynn, where he received a friendly welcome. There he became sick on October 9 or 10, apparently with dysentery, a disease affecting the intestinal tract. Some reports said he ate too many peaches and drank too much cider. Despite his illness, he continued moving through the eastern countryside.

This thirteenth-century limestone effigy of King John rests on top of his tomb in Worcester Cathedral.

And then, suddenly, John stopped his constant travels. In Newark, on the night of October 18, 1216, King John died.

DEATH OF A REBELLION

Many people in England may have cheered the king's sudden death, but they did not expect it. Neither King John's friends nor enemies had a plan for this particular outcome. John's remaining allies and servants buried the dead king at Worcester Cathedral. The loyalists then retrieved John's nine-year-old son Henry from his hiding

This illustration based on a thirteenth-century English manuscript shows Henry III's coronation, although Henry is portrayed as much older than nine.

place in a castle in southwestern England. At nearby Gloucester, on October 28, 1216, they conducted a coronation ceremony and proclaimed the boy the new monarch, King Henry III.

Since such a young boy could not rule, a committee of counselors took on the job of acting for him. William Marshal, the longtime ally of King John, was chief among these counselors. Two weeks after Henry III's coronation, on November 12, 1216, Marshal reissued the Runnymede charter. The reissued charter included some important revisions. Most significantly, it deleted the clauses relating to the commission of twenty-five barons. The commission seemed so incompatible with a king's authority that Marshal and other senior counselors thought it best not to revive it.

The reissue of the charter, coupled with the death of King John, took the wind out of the rebels' sails. At the same time, it marked the beginning of the end for Prince Louis in England. With the new king embracing the charter, the rebel barons lost much of the reason for their rebellion. Most of the rebel barons seemed to recognize that the commission of twenty-five barons was an unworkable experiment and did not fight for it. In addition, many people did not want to deny the innocent Henry his rightful inheritance. After all, Henry was entitled to the throne under ancient custom. Louis was a foreign royal whom the barons had called in as a last resort.

And so, practically overnight, the barons' enthusiasm for their foreign king weakened. More and more of the rebels came to support Henry III. To defend his supposed English crown, Louis had to bring in additional soldiers from France. This action only underlined his shrinking stature in England. After losing battles to armies that pledged their loyalty to King Henry III, Prince Louis gave up the fight. In September 1217, he sailed back to France.

The rebellion was over. The war was over. Neither the rebel nor the loyalist side had achieved decisive military victory. But by the end, there were no longer two sides. There were simply the barons of England, once again paying homage to a single king. And there was the charter.

EPILOGUE
MAGNA CARTA COMES TO LIFE

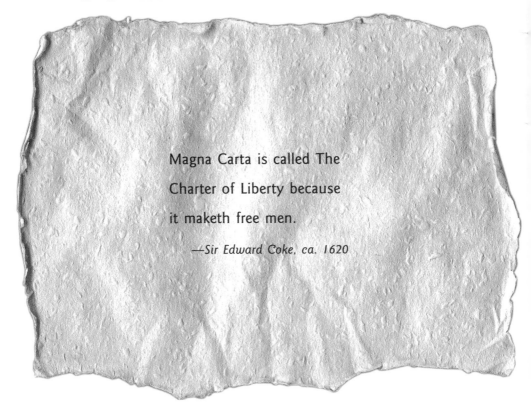

Magna Carta is called The
Charter of Liberty because
it maketh free men.

—*Sir Edward Coke, ca. 1620*

The death of King John could easily have been the death of the Magna Carta. The rebellious barons, after all, had not targeted the monarchy or the principles of taxation and royal fees. Their displeasure was aimed at King John personally. Their disgust with him was so great that they were willing to replace him with an unproven French prince.

With John dead, the target of the barons' displeasure

was gone. The barons had begun their protests with pleas to bring back the (mostly mythical) good old days before John came to the throne. It was smart politics for William Marshal to try to win back the barons' loyalty by reissuing the Runnymede charter after young King Henry III's coronation. After that, William Marshal could have let the matter rest. The charter could have gone the way of coronation charters of kings past—meaning it could have amounted to nice words that did not restrain a king from doing as he pleased.

Instead, Marshal and Henry III's other advisers took a different route. They kept the charter alive. A year after the first reissue of the charter, William Marshal issued another version of the charter, on November 6, 1217. This time, he removed the clauses that dealt with the forest. To address complaints about the forest laws, Marshal issued a separate charter, so there were two charters. To distinguish one from the other, new names were needed. One of them became known as the Charter of the Forest. The other, longer, one was called the Great Charter—*Magna Carta*.

SUBJECT TO CHANGE

William Marshal did not leave a detailed explanation of why he chose to embrace the Runnymede charter in this way. But the reissues suggest that he (and probably others) saw the charter as something more valuable than just a failed peace treaty. For Marshal did not simply re-publish the 1215 charter without any thought. Rather, he made changes in the text that showed that people continued to think about how the ideas set out in the charter would actually apply in the real world.

For example, in 1215 the charter said that if a nobleman's heirs were children when he died, those heirs could obtain their father's land without having to pay a relief fee when they came "of age"—that is, when they became adults (Clause 3). The question of when these heirs were old enough to claim their land was not answered in 1215. The 1216 reissue was more specific: an heir became "of age" when he turned twenty-one. (By definition, an heir was male.)

In the 1217 charter, Marshal reconsidered the king's promise in Clause 18 of the original charter. This referred to the call to send royal judges out to the counties four times each year to hear cases. It had become clear by that time that there were not enough judges to make appearances four times a year. In the 1217 charter, then, Marshal changed Clause 18 to reflect this reality. At most, the revised Clause 18 promised, royal judges would hold court in each county once a year.

Defining when a person came of age and specifying how frequently royal judges would hold court did not amount to huge transformations. What these and other refinements in the 1216 and 1217 reissues showed was that the charter was not a fixed, unchangeable document. It was not merely of historical or symbolic interest. King John was dead, but the charter continued living and changing as people continued to develop ideas about the relationship of a ruler to citizens and to law.

LAW OF THE LAND

By the mid-1200s, the Magna Carta was on its way to becoming a permanent fixture in the English political landscape. In part, this may have been because of the stirring history surrounding the charter, particularly the bitter conflict between King John and the barons. People

A GLOBAL CHARTER

The Magna Carta was an English creation, but its influence extended beyond the boundaries of that country and its American colonies. In 1948 the General Assembly of United Nations, an international organization whose membership includes nearly all the world's nations, adopted the Universal Declaration of Human Rights. The Declaration sets out fundamental rights and freedoms that all people should enjoy. Many of these rights and freedoms echo the principles of the Magna Carta, including the following sections of the Declaration:

Article 9.
No one shall be subjected to arbitrary arrest, detention or exile.

Article 10.
Everyone is entitled in full equality to a fair and public hearing by an independent and impartial tribunal, in the determination of his rights and obligations and of any criminal charge against him.

may have clung to the charter because it commemorated such an epic event in their history. But the Magna Carta also may have gained acceptance because it reflected ideas taking shape in society at large.

A well-known law book written in the mid-1200s provides a mirror of these ideas. Written in Latin, it was called *De legibus et consuetudinibus Angliae* (*On the Laws and Customs of England*). People said it was the work of Henry of Bratton (also known as Bracton), a judge in the royal courts from 1247 to 1257. His ambitious work attempted to describe all of English law at the time.

Significantly, Bracton said that under the laws and customs of England, the king was not above the law. In other words, although a king was superior to all others in the land, even he had to follow certain rules and limits on his power. "The king must not be under man but under God and under the law," Bracton wrote, "because law makes the king."

In the time of the Magna Carta and half a century later, in Bracton's time, the idea that the king was subject to law was part wishful thinking and part statement of actual fact. Kings of that era did not wish to give up their powers. But times were changing, and Bracton and documents such as the Magna Carta were part of the change. Kings and those who were subject to their rule still argued about how far the king could go in enforcing his absolute will and power. The Magna Carta did not stop the argument. But beginning in 1215, it was a part of the argument.

LIKE FATHER, LIKE SON?

When he was old enough to rule in his own right, Henry III encountered as many problems as his father had in keeping the loyalty of the English barons. Like King John, Henry ran into trouble when he sought to extract higher and higher taxes to finance wars and other projects. In 1260 Henry's actions sparked a new revolt. The conflict soon ripened into all-out war between the king's soldiers and the forces of a new generation of rebelling barons.

For a time, Henry was forced to share his powers with a council of advisers, made up of barons who both supported and opposed him. At one point, Henry's brother-in-law, a baron named Simon de Montfort, took over the king's authority almost entirely. To shore up his own support, in 1265 Montfort held a meeting of

The barons, led by Simon de Montfort, approach Henry III in 1264, shortly before openly revolting. This painting is by nineteenth-century French artist Georges Rouget.

representatives of smaller landholders, churchmen, and townspeople, in addition to the barons, to discuss matters of government. Not a legislature in the modern sense, this gathering was, in a way, a preview of the English Parliament. The Montfort-controlled monarchy also decreed, in 1265, that the Magna Carta should be read aloud twice a year in the county courts. Translators translated the Latin texts into English and French, and those versions were read in courts throughout England.

This medieval French manuscript illustration shows Edward I on his throne.

Simon de Montfort's experiment in governing did not last long. Later in 1265, Henry's son, Edward, led forces to defeat Montfort's soldiers. Montfort was killed in the process. But once Edward took the throne in 1272 as King Edward I, he continued the practice of convening parliaments.

And twenty-five years later, in 1297, King Edward I publicly reconfirmed the Magna Carta. He was not acting out of the goodness of his heart. Rather, by this time, Edward (like his father and grandfather) had gotten himself involved in too many expensive wars. Barons, churchmen, and parliament were balking at Edward's expenses. By reconfirming the Magna Carta, Edward was redeeming himself, at least in part, in the eyes of people whose support he needed. The charter was copied into the official statute book. The Magna Carta officially became a part of the law of the land.

JUSTICE FOR ALL

Years passed. Kings lived and died, and the Magna Carta lived on. By the 1300s, England had an organized legislative assembly—the Parliament. Members of Parliament required government officials to swear an oath to respect the charter. In Parliament itself, the Magna Carta was read aloud every year and confirmed by the members.

In the 1300s, Parliament also took Clause 39 of the Magna Carta and turned it into separate specific statutes. In doing this, the lawmakers changed and expanded the charter's meaning. In the 1215 version of the charter, Clause 39 read as follows:

"No *free man* shall be seized or imprisoned, or stripped of his rights or possessions, or outlawed or exiled, or deprived of his standing in any other way, nor will we proceed with force against him, or send others to do so, *except by the lawful judgement of his equals* [also translated as "peers"] or by *the law of the land.*"

First, Parliament interpreted "except by the lawful judgement of his equals" (or "peers") to mean "except by trial by peers." In this way, Parliament read into Clause

39 a requirement that legal proceedings against a person must involve a trial by peers, or trial by jury. Next, for "law of the land," Parliament substituted "due process of law." This emphasized that legal action against a person must follow fair legal rules of procedure. That is, a person could not be punished or deprived of his property without "due process of law"—without fair and regular legal procedures in courts.

Finally, a statute of 1354 abandoned "no free man" and substituted "no man of whatever estate or condition he may be." Through this change, Parliament extended the rights of trial by jury and due process of law to all men, including villeins and people without landholdings. (Women were also understood to be included in the scope of Clause 39.)

By the middle of the fourteenth century, then, the justice clause of the Magna Carta had been reinterpreted well beyond its original meaning. The authors of Runnymede were gone, and new generations of leaders had taken their place. They had new ideas about government and justice. And so they transformed Clause 39 from just another section of the Magna Carta to something far more significant. It became the controlling principle for legal process in England.

SACRED PLEDGE

Along with new generations of nonroyal leaders, new generations of kings took their places in England as well. They were still jealous of their powers, even while they

paid lip service to the
Magna Carta. In the early
1600s, the changing ideas
of some leaders in
Parliament and the more
traditional ideas of the
kings came into sharp
conflict. Sir Edward Coke
was the chief proponent
of the idea that the
Magna Carta gave
citizens the right to be
free from royal excesses.
Coke served as attorney

Sir Edward Coke

general, solicitor general, chief justice, and member of
Parliament in England. Despite these high positions, Coke
ended up in jail for his outspokenness about the Magna
Carta and against King James I.

Coke continued speaking out and writing about the
Magna Carta until he died in 1634. He was unwavering
in his view that under the Magna Carta, no person, not
even a king, was above the law. Everyone, including kings
and governments, must act in accordance with the laws
of the land. Coke also insisted that the Magna Carta
stood for the proposition that laws must be fair and good
to be valid and that laws could not take away basic
individual liberties. In Coke's writings, the Magna Carta
was once again transformed. It became a guarantee of
individual liberty—an almost sacred pledge that the
government would not trample the people's freedoms.

A REVOLUTION'S INSPIRATION

Coke's writings did not create an immediate change in
the behavior or ideas of later kings of England. However,
his views took hold among many lawyers, scholars, and
members of Parliament concerned about excessive royal
authority. These ideas influenced the development of
England's unwritten constitutional law. And they were
reflected in England's common law—that is, law that is
made by judges in their rulings in individual court cases.

A century after Coke, in the mid-1700s, another great
legal scholar, William Blackstone, wrote a pair of highly
influential works. They were the *Commentaries on the
Laws of England* (1765–1769) and another study, *The
Great Charter and the Charter of the Forest* (1759).
Blackstone agreed with Coke's interpretation of the
Magna Carta. Their ideas echoed across the Atlantic
Ocean, where they were music to the ears of American
colonists struggling against oppressive British rule under
King George III. When the colonists announced in 1776
that they were breaking away from Britain to form a new
country, they did so in language that reflected their
familiarity with Blackstone's and Coke's Magna Carta.

Among other things, the Declaration of Independence
noted with displeasure the king's approval of laws that
imposed "taxes on us without our Consent" and deprived
people of "the benefits of Trial by Jury." The rebelling
American colonists did not directly quote the Magna
Carta in their Declaration of Independence. But many of
their ideas about what a king was not entitled to do
echoed the complaints of the barons of Runnymede.

The American Declaration of Independence was issued on July 4, 1776. Thomas Jefferson, who drafted the declaration for the Continental Congress, wrote the document with the idea that rulers are subject to the rule of law. Fifty-six members of the Continental Congress signed the Declaration before it was sent to King George III.

MAGNA MASSACHUSETTS

Although most American colonists were not trained in British law, they knew about the Magna Carta. After the first battles of the American Revolution (1775–1783) against England had been fought in the two small Massachusetts towns of Lexington and Concord, the rebelling patriots of Massachusetts adopted a new seal for their colony. The new seal pictured a militiaman with a sword in one hand—and the Magna Carta in the other. The famous Boston silversmith and patriot Paul Revere engraved the seal, which was used by Massachusetts until 1780.

CONSTITUTIONAL INFLUENCES

In 1783 the American colonists won their freedom from England and turned to the task of writing a basic law, or constitution, for their new country. The authors of the U.S. Constitution and Bill of Rights (the first ten amendments to the Constitution) continued to invoke principles of the Magna Carta, as those principles had expanded over the centuries. For example, the Magna Carta provided in Clauses 12 and 14 that taxes required "the general consent of the realm." In the Constitution, the idea that the people must consent to taxes was reflected in Article I, Section 8. That provision granted Congress, as the representative of the people, the power to "To lay and collect Taxes, Duties, Imposts and Excises." The president of the United States, like the king of England under the Magna Carta, was not allowed to impose taxes without the consent of the people.

But it was Clauses 39 and 40 of the Magna Carta that exerted the greatest influence on the new nation's Constitution. The Fifth Amendment to the Constitution guaranteed that "no person shall be . . . deprived of life, liberty, or property, without due process of law." The Sixth Amendment guaranteed people accused of crimes the right to a "speedy and public trial, by an impartial jury of the State and district wherein the crime shall have been committed." The Seventh Amendment insisted that "the right of trial by jury shall be preserved" in noncriminal, or civil, lawsuits as well. All these amendments bore the undeniable influences of Clause 39: "No free man shall be seized or imprisoned, or stripped of his rights or possessions, or outlawed or exiled, or deprived of his standing in any other way . . . except by the lawful judgement of his equals or by the law of the land." And they were influenced by Clause 40 as well: "To no one will we sell, to no one deny or delay right or justice."

SYMBOL OF LIBERTY

In 1863, after 566 years as part of the official written law of England, Parliament removed the Magna Carta from its official statute book. Most of the charter's provisions had grown outdated and irrelevant, relating as they did to the intricacies of medieval property holding. However, three provisions remained. One guaranteed the freedom

RHYMES FOR RUNNYMEDE

British writer Rudyard Kipling (1865–1936) wrote a poem extolling the Magna Carta. It was called "What Say the Reeds at Runnymede?" An excerpt follows:

At Runnymede, at Runnymede,
　　Oh, hear the reeds at Runnymede:
"You musn't sell, delay, deny,
　　A freeman's right or liberty.
It wakes the stubborn Englishry,
　　We saw 'em roused at Runnymede!
. . . .
At Runnymede, at Runnymede,
　　Your rights were won at Runnymede!
No freeman shall be fined or bound,
　　Or dispossessed of freehold ground,
Except by lawful judgment found
　　And passed upon him by his peers.
Forget not, after all these years,
　　The Charter signed at Runnymede.

of the English (Anglican) church (Clause 1 of the 1215 charter). A second confirmed, without specifying, the traditional privileges of London and other cities (Clause 13 of the 1215 charter). And the third remaining provision was the descendant of Clauses 39 and 40, which had become so famous over the centuries.

Whether the Magna Carta remained on Britain's statute book or not, it could not be erased from British law. Similarly, the Magna Carta remains very much a part of U.S. law, even though it was never formally part of the written statutes of the United States. The charter's ideas—or, more precisely, the ideas people have attributed to it over the centuries—have become ingrained in society, law, and politics in both countries. From a failed peace treaty, the Magna Carta became a symbol of individual liberty and rights and of the limits of government authority. The barons and King John may not have intended to change world history—but that is what they did.

PRIMARY SOURCE RESEARCH

To learn about historical events, people study many sources, such as books, websites, newspaper articles, photographs, and paintings. These sources can be separated into two general categories—primary sources and secondary sources.

A primary source is the record of an eyewitness. Primary sources provide firsthand accounts about a person or event. Examples include diaries, letters, autobiographies, speeches, newspapers, and oral history interviews. Libraries, archives, historical societies, and museums often have primary sources available on-site or on the Internet.

A secondary source is published information that was researched, collected, and written or otherwise created by someone who was not an eyewitness. These authors or artists use primary sources and other secondary sources in their research, but they interpret and arrange the source material in their own works. Secondary sources include history books, novels, biographies, movies, documentaries, and magazines. Libraries and museums are filled with secondary sources.

After finding primary and secondary sources, authors and historians must evaluate them. They may ask questions such as: Who created this document? What is this person's point of view? What biases might this person have? How trustworthy is this document? Just because a person was an eyewitness to an event does not mean that person recorded the whole truth about that event. For example, a soldier describing a battle might depict only the heroic actions of his unit and only the brutal behavior of the enemy. An account from a soldier on the opposing side might portray the same battle very differently. When sources disagree, researchers must decide through additional study which explanation makes the most sense. For this reason, historians consult a variety of primary and secondary sources. Then they can draw their own conclusions.

The Pivotal Moments in History series takes readers on a journey to important junctures in history that shaped our world as we know it today. Each event has been researched using both primary and secondary sources to enhance the awareness of the complexities of the materials and rich stories from which we draw our understanding of our shared history.

LEARNING ABOUT THE MAGNA CARTA

Ever since King John affixed his royal seal on the Magna Carta nearly eight hundred years ago, succeeding generations have been unable to resist the urge to dress up the yellowing old document. This is not to say that anyone has actually tampered with the original sheets of parchment. No, the four remaining original copies of the Magna Carta from 1215 are carefully protected in Britain. Two are in the British Library in London, one is at

Lincoln Cathedral, and another is at Salisbury Cathedral. But almost from the time the Magna Carta came into existence, people began to clothe it in meanings that those who created it never intended.

In modern times, the Magna Carta is famous as one of the earliest statements of the rights of individuals to be free from unjust governments. Respected legal scholars have analyzed the importance of the Magna Carta to constitutional government—that is, to government that is created by free people and is answerable to them. The Magna Carta did, eventually, take on this meaning. But it didn't start out that way.

And so, to uncover the original meaning of the Magna Carta and to understand its history, a researcher must actually turn away from some of the most famous documents that have commented on it. These include Sir Edward Coke's analysis of the Magna Carta, in his work titled *Institutes of the Laws of England*, written in the 1600s. Coke was among the greatest advocates of the view that the Magna Carta is a guarantee of just laws and government. His book is treated as a primary source in the field of constitutional law. But to read Coke on the Magna Carta is to get a view of history that is colored by the politics and social conditions of the 1600s. Similarly, writers from the 1700s, 1800s, and 1900s have also offered views of the Magna Carta that reflected the concerns of their own times.

Turning to primary sources written around the time of King John as a way to understand the Magna Carta presents different challenges. The key primary documents themselves can leave researchers perplexed. The Magna Carta, for example, was written in Latin. Translating the Latin into English or other modern languages is not the challenge for historians and writers. The challenge is in understanding what people in 1215 did with the Latin document. Latin was the language of educated people at the time. Not everybody—not even all barons and nobles—could read or understand Latin. After King John and the barons agreed on the Magna Carta, copies of it were distributed across the land with instructions that sheriffs or others should hold public readings of the charter. It is unlikely that these public readings were conducted in Latin. Probably the readers delivered a version of the charter translated into the local language (either a form of English or of French). But one cannot know for certain.

Besides two copies of the Magna Carta, the British Library also holds the Articles of the Barons. The document is undated but is assumed to predate the Magna Carta, at least by some days. It appears to be a draft of the Magna Carta. Perhaps the barons drew it up among themselves and thrust it before the king in the field at Runnymede where the opposing parties met in June 1215. Perhaps the barons and the king (or the king's men) wrote the Articles of the Barons together, before gathering at Runnymede for a final ceremony. Under one assumption, the barons are seen as making their demands of the king, in a rather dramatic fashion. Under the other assumption, the Articles of the Barons and the resulting Magna Carta appear to be more the products of cooperation and negotiation. Again, no one really knows which is the more accurate picture.

Still, other primary sources dating from the Magna Carta era—such as records, accounts, chronicles, and letters—allow historians to re-create many of the important events leading up to and after Runnymede with some certainty. Much information about daily life in King John's England is contained in official records compiled by royal officials. These include the Pipe Rolls (accounts of money collected by the crown from subjects), Charter Rolls (formal documents in which the king granted land or privileges), Patent Rolls (letters announcing a royal decision on a variety of matters), and more. Many of these records are preserved in Britain's National Archives. Some are available on the Internet. They provide a detailed glimpse into legal and economic relationships at the time of the Magna Carta, which allows historians to better understand the issues that resulted in the Magna Carta.

For greater insight into the events surrounding the Magna Carta, historians and researchers also refer to the writings of various people who witnessed the era. Invaluable as these writings are, they must be read with caution. Some writers were more interested in putting forth their points of view than in presenting unbiased history. Roger of Wendover's book *Flowers of History* portrayed pretty much everything King John did as cruel, deceitful, and worse. Wendover detested the king, and Wendover's opinions surely slanted his accounts of the events of 1215. Another source of information about the era is *The History of William the Marshal,* an anonymous thirteenth-century poem of nearly twenty thousand lines. It is a useful historical text, but a modern reader must keep in mind that its writer had a motive—he was hired to write a tribute to William Marshal, Earl of Pembroke. The point of the poem was to portray Marshal in a favorable light.

Anyone learning and writing about the Magna Carta in modern times must accept that significant gaps exist in the history of the document and the times. Even the most unbiased writers necessarily choose versions of history that seem most plausible to them, in light of all the evidence. Through careful use of the available sources, a writer works to create the most accurate account possible. But in the end, history is a narrative of events. It is a story, not a science.

THE LANGUAGE OF THE MAGNA CARTA

The Magna Carta was written in Latin, a language that educated English people could read and write in 1215. Latin was the language of court and other official documents. It was, therefore, not surprising that the authors of the Magna Carta composed their work in Latin.

The original charter contained no separate clauses but rather was written as one continuous, unbroken, very long paragraph. Clause numbers are often inserted for the sake of clarity.

FINDING OUT MORE ABOUT THE MAGNA CARTA

The complete British Library English translation of the Magna Carta can be found at the British Library website, http://www.bl.uk/treasures/magnacarta/translation.html. It is also in the British Library publication, *Magna Carta: Manuscripts and Myths* (London: British Library, 2002, 49–54), by Claire Breay. The complete Latin version is reprinted in J. C. Holt, *Magna Carta,* 2nd ed. (New York: Cambridge University Press, 1992, 448–472). The Latin version can also be found at the Grand [Masonic] Lodge of British Columbia and Yukon website, http://freemasonry.bcy.ca/texts/magnacarta.html.

PRIMARY SOURCE DOCUMENT

This is one of the four surviving copies of the 1215 Magna Carta. It is housed at the British Library in London.

EXCERPTS FROM THE LATIN MAGNA CARTA

The Latin version is taken from an original charter held by the British Library in London, England. The English translation is also from the British Library. The first section set out here is the introductory clause of the charter, in which King John is introduced and the nobles involved in the making of the Magna Carta are identified by name. This is followed by several of the most famous clauses.

PORTIONS OF THE MAGNA CARTA IN LATIN

Johannes del gracia rex Anglie, dominus Hibernie, dux
Normannie, Aquitannie et comes Andegavie, archiepiscopis,
episcopis, abbatibus, comitibus, baronibus, justiciariis, forestariis,
vicecomitibus, prepositis, ministris et omnibus ballivis et fidelibus
suis salutem. Sciatis nos intuitu Dei et pro salute anime nostre et
omnium antecessorum et heredum nostrorum ad honorem Dei et
exaltacionem sancte Ecclesie, et emendacionem regni nostri, per
consilium venerabilium patrum nostrorum, Stephani
Cantuariensis archiepiscopi tocius Anglie primatis et sancte
Romane ecclesie cardinalis, Henrici Dublinensis archiepiscopi,
Willelmi Londoniensis, Petri Wintoniensis, Joscelini Bathoniensis
et Glastoniensis, Hugonis Lincolniensis, Walteri Wygorniensis,
Willelmi Coventrensis, et Benedicti Roffensis, episcoporum;
magistri Pandulfi domini pape subdiaconi et familiaris, fratris
Aymerici magistri milicie Templi in Anglia; et nobilium virorum
Willelmi Mariscalli comitis Penbrocie, Willelmi comitis
Sarrisberie, Willelmi comitis Warennie, Willelmi comitis
Arundellie, Alani de Galeweya constabularii Scocie, Warini filii
Geroldi, Petri filii Hereberti, Huberti de Burgo senescalli Pictavie,
Hugonis de Nevilla, Mathei filli Hereberti, Thome Basset, Alani
Basset, Philippi de Albiniaco, Roberti de Roppel', Johannis
Mariscalli, Johannis filii Hugonis et aliorum fidelium nostrorum:

(See pages 134–135 for clauses.)

AN ENGLISH TRANSLATION

JOHN, by the grace of God King of England, Lord of Ireland, Duke of Normandy and Aquitaine, and Count of Anjou, to his archbishops, bishops, abbots, earls, barons, justices, foresters, sheriffs, stewards, servants, and to all his officials and loyal subjects, Greeting. KNOW THAT BEFORE GOD, for the health of our soul and those of our ancestors and heirs, to the honour of God, the exaltation of the holy Church, and the better ordering of our kingdom, at the advice of our reverend fathers Stephen, archbishop of Canterbury, primate of all England, and cardinal of the holy Roman Church, Henry archbishop of Dublin, William bishop of London, Peter bishop of Winchester, Jocelin bishop of Bath and Glastonbury, Hugh bishop of Lincoln, Walter Bishop of Worcester, William bishop of Coventry, Benedict bishop of Rochester, Master Pandulf subdeacon and member of the papal household, Brother Aymeric master of the knighthood of the Temple in England, William Marshal earl of Pembroke, William earl of Salisbury, William earl of Warren, William earl of Arundel, Alan de Galloway constable of Scotland, Warin Fitz Gerald, Peter Fitz Herbert, Hubert de Burgh seneschal of Poitou, Hugh de Neville, Matthew Fitz Herbert, Thomas Basset, Alan Basset, Philip Daubeny, Robert de Roppeley, John Marshal, John Fitz Hugh, and other loyal subjects:

(See pages 134–135 for clauses.)

133

39. Nullus liber homo capiatur, vel imprisonetur, aut disseisiatur, aut utlagetur, aut exuletur, aut aliquo modo destruatur, nec super cum ibimus, nec super cum mittemus, nisi per legale judicium parium suorum vel per legem terre.

40. Nulli vendemus, nulli negabimus aut differemus rectum aut justiciam.

63. Quare volumus et firmiter precipimus quod Anglicana ecclesia libera sit et quod homines in regno nostro habeant et teneant omnes prefatas libertates, Jura, et concessiones, bene et in pace, libere et quiete, plene et integre, sibi et heredibus suis, de nobis et heredibus nostris, in omnibus rebus et locis, in perpetuum, sicut predictum est. Juratum est autem tam ex parte nostra quam ex parte baronum, quod hec omnia supradicta bona fide et sine malo ingenio observabuntur. Testibus supradictis et multis aliis. Data per manum nostram in prato quod vocatur Ronimed inter Windlesoram et Stanes, quinto dccimo die Junii, anno regni nostri decimo septimo.

39. No free man shall be seized or imprisoned, or stripped of his rights or possessions, or outlawed or exiled, or deprived of his standing in any other way, nor will we proceed with force against him, or send others to do so, except by the lawful judgement of his equals or by the law of the land.

40. To no one will we sell, to no one deny or delay right or justice.

63. IT IS ACCORDINGLY OUR WISH AND COMMAND that the English Church shall be free, and that men in our kingdom shall have and keep all these liberties, rights, and concessions, well and peaceably in their fulness and entirety for them and their heirs, of us and our heirs, in all things and all places for ever. Both we and the barons have sworn that all this shall be observed in good faith and without deceit. Witness the above-mentioned people and many others.
Given by our hand in the meadow that is called Runnymede, between Windsor and Staines, on the fifteenth day of June in the seventeenth year of our reign [that is, 1215].

TIMELINE

1066   William of Normandy, also known as William the Conqueror, invades England and crowns himself king. He establishes a monarchy and requires that nobles pay him high taxes and other fees as a condition of holding property.

1100   King Henry I, youngest son of William the Conqueror, takes the throne of England and issues his Charter of Liberties, or Coronation Charter.

1154   Henry II becomes king of England and enlarges the empire he has inherited.

1189   Upon the death of Henry II, his oldest surviving son, Richard I, becomes king. He promptly goes off to fight in the Crusades. His ministers at home work hard to keep taxes and fees flowing into the royal treasury.

This print shows King Richard in the Crusades.

1192 Returning home from the Crusades, King Richard I is captured by Leopold, Duke of Austria, who turns him over to Emperor Henry VI. Richard's ministers get to work extracting even more taxes from the population, to raise money for the king's ransom. Richard's younger brother John plots to take over his brother's throne.

1194 King Richard's ministers finally raised enough ransom to pay for his release, and he returns to England. John abandons his plot.

1199 Richard dies and his brother John becomes king.

1203 Arthur of Brittany, challenger to King John's throne, is murdered. Many suspect John of ordering the killing.

Arthur of Brittany is murdered at Rouen, France.

| 1204 | After a series of battles with King Philip Augustus of France, King John loses Normandy and nearly all the rest of his French territories. John immediately starts pressuring English nobles for more money to rebuild the royal treasury, which has been depleted by war. |

This fourteenth-century French manuscript illustration shows King John paying homage to King Philip Augustus after losing Normandy.

| 1207 | Pope Innocent III names Stephen Langton the archbishop of Canterbury, setting off a conflict with King John, who refuses to let Langton take office. |
| 1208 | The pope imposes an interdict on England, under which priests are forbidden to conduct important |

	religious ceremonies in England. King John retaliates by seizing church property.
1209	The pope excommunicates King John.
1213	Facing a threat of invasion from France, King John reverses his opposition to Stephen Langton and agrees to submit his kingdom to the authority of Pope Innocent III.
1214	After sailing to France intent on recapturing Normandy, King John and his allies are decisively defeated by King Philip Augustus of France. This is the end of the English Empire in France.
DECEMBER 1214	English barons, disgusted with King John's endless pressures on them for money to support his wars, demand changes in royal administration.
JANUARY 1215	At a meeting in London, barons threaten war if King John does not change his ways. The king promises to meet the barons again in April.
APRIL 26, 1215	The barons show up for their appointment with King John. The king fails to attend.

MAY 1215	The barons renounce their loyalty to King John. They take over the city of London without a fight and make it the headquarters of their rebellion. At the end of the month, King John formally rejects the barons' demands for change.
JUNE 1215	Despite uncompromising words on both sides, supporters of both the king and rebels meet at Runnymede to negotiate, beginning around June 10. A list of demands is produced. By June 15, the list has been shaped into a charter. The final charter, the Magna Carta, is produced on June 19 and agreed to by both sides.

This is a nineteenth-century depiction of King John signing the Magna Carta at Runnymede.

140

JULY 1215	King John sends a message to Pope Innocent III asking that he declare the Magna Carta invalid.
AUGUST 1215	The pope announces that the Magna Carta is illegal.
SEPTEMBER 1215	The barons and King John are at war.
MAY 22, 1216	Prince Louis of France lands in England and is crowned king by rebel barons.
OCTOBER 18, 1216	King John dies.
OCTOBER 28, 1216	John's loyalists crown his nine-year-old son, Henry III, the new king of England.
NOVEMBER 12, 1216	Henry III's chief adviser, William Marshal, reissues the Magna Carta.
1217	Abandoned by the barons, Prince Louis sails back to France in September. On November 6, William Marshal issues another version of the Magna Carta.
FEBRUARY 11, 1225	The Magna Carta is reissued under the seal of King Henry III.

141

GLOSSARY

ARCHBISHOP: a high-ranking bishop

BAILIFF: a person who manages an estate or farm for a landowner

BURGESS: a citizen of an English town

CHARTER: a written contract

COMMONER: a person who is not of noble rank

FEALTY: fidelity; loyalty; devotion; allegiance of a tenant toward a lord

FEUDALISM: a term used to describe a formal system of relationships between kings, nobles, and their many subjects. Recent scholarly studies have cast doubt on whether or not any such rigid system of feudalism ever truly existed.

HEIR: one who inherits or is entitled to inherit property, rank, title, or office, or a combination of these

HOMAGE: a ceremony in which a person acknowledges himself as subservient to his lord or king

MANOR: an estate; also, a house or hall on an estate

NOBLEMAN: a man of noble rank

PARISH: a unit of area in medieval England

PEASANT: farmers or laborers

REEVE: a person responsible for overseeing a noble's holdings

SCUTAGE: a tax in lieu of military service

TENANT: one who holds or possesses real estate but doesn't own it

TRENCHER: a platter for serving food

VILLEIN: a peasant who was legally restricted to work a lord's land and to follow his various rules

WHO'S WHO?

ELEANOR OF AQUITAINE (CA. 1122–1204) The wife of King Henry II, Eleanor had previously been married to King Louis VII of France. While married to Louis VII, in 1147, Eleanor traveled thousands of miles with him and his French soldiers into present-day Turkey to fight in the Crusades. Louis VII and Eleanor divorced in 1152, and within two months, Eleanor married twenty-year-old Henry, who was eleven years younger than she. Eleanor's landholdings greatly enlarged Henry II's empire in western France. King Henry II and Eleanor had seven children— three girls and four boys. Eleanor was known to have a willful, strong personality. In part because she wished to have more authority in her own region of Aquitaine, she encouraged her boys, when in their late teens, to rebel against Henry II. The king tried to control her by putting her in jail, but still Henry II had to fight off rebellions from his sons for nearly half of his reign. Eleanor remained in jail for fifteen years, until she was in her sixties. When Henry II died in 1189, Richard I became king and released his mother from jail. Even into her old age, she worked to support Richard I's reign, especially when Richard faced a plot by his younger brother (Eleanor's youngest son), John, to take over the throne. After Richard's death, John became king. Eleanor died during John's reign.

WILLIAM BLACKSTONE (1723–1780) Blackstone was an

unremarkable lawyer in eighteenth-century England when, at the age of thirty, he decided to prepare a series of lectures on the common law of England (that is, the law based on customs and court decisions). These lectures, which shed light on a subject that many people otherwise had found inaccessible and boring, brought Blackstone fame and admiration. He continued rewriting and expanding the lectures, until they became a four-volume encyclopedia of English law, called *Commentaries on the Law of England*. The ideas expressed in the *Commentaries* about the supremacy of the law and the rights and liberties of English citizens influenced the American colonists who declared their independence from Britain in 1776. Later, Blackstone became a member of Parliament, a solicitor general, and a judge. He also wrote a book about the Magna Carta.

EDWARD COKE (1552–1634) Coke served as a member of Parliament, attorney general, solicitor general, and chief justice of England during his long career. He became most famous for his interpretations of the Magna Carta and views on English common law. In Coke's view, the Magna Carta reflected the common law principle that even the king was not above the law. He also asserted that the people of England enjoyed certain basic freedoms, including the right to be free from unreasonable royal actions.

HENRY II (1133–1189) Henry II, who was raised in the French province of Anjou, became king of England after years of conflict between his mother, Matilda (daughter of King Henry I), and King Stephen. Finally, when Stephen died in 1154, Henry II was crowned king. As king, Henry II greatly expanded his empire, through military action and marriage to Eleanor of Aquitaine. He centralized royal authority during his reign, especially by strengthening the power of the royal courts. Henry II was plagued by rebellions within his own family, with his wife and sons (two of whom, Richard and John, later inherited his throne), all fighting against him at one time or another. He also engaged in a historical quarrel with the Roman Catholic Church over the power of the church courts and other issues. His disagreements with his former close friend, Archbishop of Canterbury Thomas Becket, led some of Henry's knights to murder Becket in his chambers at Canterbury Cathedral in 1170. Henry II later apologized for the murder, and the church declared Becket a saint, Saint Thomas of Canterbury.

INNOCENT III (CA. 1160–1216) Born Lotario de'Conti di

Degni, the son of a Roman nobleman, Pope Innocent III became head of the Roman Catholic Church in 1198. His years as pope (1198–1216) coincided nearly exactly with King John's reign in England (1199–1216). From 1208 to 1213, Innocent III placed penalties on England and on King John personally, as punishment for John's refusal

to accept the pope's choice as archbishop of Canterbury. When John relented, the pope lifted his penalties and also supported John in his struggles with the barons of England that led to the Magna Carta.

JOHN (1167–1216) The youngest son of King Henry II and

Eleanor of Aquitaine, John became king in 1199 after the death of his older brother Richard I. As a boy and young man, he was known as John Lackland, since his father—who otherwise favored him—was obliged by custom to leave his vast landholdings to his older sons. John's reign was rocked by conflicts with the Roman Catholic Church, with France, and with the nobles of England. After suffering military defeats that cost him England's landholdings in France, John then had to deal with his barons, who were unhappy after years of high taxes and unpopular wars. Eventually, he agreed to the Magna Carta in 1215 and died a year later.

LOUIS OF FRANCE (1187–1226) The son of King Philip Augustus (Philip II) of France, Prince Louis was briefly made king of England in 1216 by the barons who rebelled against King John. When John died, his loyalists declared his son Henry III as the new king. Before long, the rebel barons dumped Louis, who returned to France. In 1223 he ascended to the throne of France following the death of his father, becoming King Louis VIII. However, he only ruled for three years, dying of dysentery on his way home to Paris after fighting battles in southern France to bring that region firmly under French rule. Louis was married to a granddaughter of King Henry II of England, with whom he had twelve children.

WILLIAM MARSHAL (1146–1219) William Marshal, Earl of Pembroke, was one of King John's most steadfast loyalists during John's years of struggles with the barons of England. He played a key role in the negotiations that led to the Magna Carta in 1215. After King John's death, Marshal became the chief adviser to John's son, King Henry III, effectively ruling for the child-king. Marshal reissued the Magna Carta in 1216 and 1217, helping to cement the document in English law and society. As a younger man, Marshal was famed for his athletic abilities, including his talent for throwing stones long distances.

PHILIP AUGUSTUS (1165–1223) Philip Augustus, also known as Philip II, was king of France from 1180 to 1223. He fought in the Crusades with England's King Richard I but otherwise devoted much of his energy to destroying Richard's empire. Philip's territorial designs on Richard's empire were probably sharpened by his personal resentments against Richard's father, King Henry II. Henry II's wife, Eleanor of Aquitaine, had previously been married to Philip Augustus's father, King Louis VII of France. In addition, Henry II was rumored to have seduced Alice, King Louis VII's daughter from his second marriage (and

Philip Augustus's sister). After Richard's death in 1199, King Philip Augustus bested Richard's brother, the new King John, in important battles in 1203–1204 and 1214. As a result of these military victories, Philip Augustus added Normandy and most of the other former English territories in western France, to his own kingdom of France.

RICHARD I (1157–1199) Richard was the third son of King Henry II and Eleanor of Aquitaine. He joined his two older brothers in a revolt against their father in 1173 and continued warring against Henry II until Henry's death in 1189. At that point, Richard became king of England and ruler of the large empire in western France and Ireland that Henry II had stitched together during his reign. Richard spent little time in England during his youth, and his monarchy did not change this pattern—he spent only one year of his ten-year reign in England. Richard's main claim to fame was as a courageous and chivalrous warrior. He earned the nickname Richard the Lion Heart when he fought in the Crusades in the early 1190s. King Richard's younger brother John plotted to take over as king when Richard was captured on his return home from the Crusades. This plot ended when Richard was released and returned to England to reclaim his throne.

SOURCE NOTES

4 Sir Edward Coke, preface to *Coke on Magna Carta, The Second Part of the Institutes of the Laws of England,* reproduction of 1797 ed. (Palmdale, CA: Omni Publications, 1998).

8 quoted in National Archives of England, Wales, and the United Kingdom, "Domesday Book," *The National Archives of England, Wales, and the United Kingdom,* n.d., http:// www.nationalarchives.gov.uk/ museum/item.asp?item_id=1. (March 27, 2007).

13 quoted in Danny Danziger and John Gillingham, *1215: The Year of Magna Carta* (New York: Simon & Schuster, 2003), 112.

24 William FitzStephen, A Description of London, translated by Stephen Alsford, *Medieval English Towns Website,* April 5, 2006, http://www.trytel.com/ ~tristan/towns/florilegium/ introduction/intro01.html (March 27, 2007).

26 Danziger and Gillingham, 13.

40 Britannia Internet Magazine. "Sources of British History:

The Charter of Liberties of King Henry I," 1997, http://www.britannia.com/ history/docs/charter.html (March 27, 2007).

43 Ibid.

43 Ibid.

54 *Internet Sacred Texts Archive,* "The Gest of Robyn Hode," Internet Sacred Texts Archive, n.d., http://www .sacred-texts.com/neu/eng/ child/ch117.htm (March 27, 2007).

58 William Shakespeare, *The Life and Death of King John,* act 2, scene 1, Available online at *Bartleby.com,* 2005, http://www.bartleby.com/70/ 2521.html (March 27, 2007).

65 Ibid., act 3, scene 4, available at *Bartleby.com,* 2005, http://www.bartleby.com/70/ 2534.html (March 27, 2007).

74 Roger of Wendover, *Flowers of History,* quoted from William Sharp McKechnie, *Magna Carta: A Commentary on the Great Charter of King John, with an Historical Introduction* (Glasgow: Maclehose, 1914), available at the Online Library of Liberty, April 20, 2004,

http://oll.libertyfund.org/
Texts/McKechnie0323/0032
_Bk.html (March 27, 2007).

78 Roger of Wendover, *Flowers
    of History*, translated by J.
    A. Giles, Vol. 2, (London:
    Henry G. Born, 1849),
    308–309, available online at
    Internet Medieval Sourcebook,
    June 1997, http://www
    .fordham.edu/halsall/source/
    wendover1215.html (March
    27, 2007).

81 British Library, "Magna
    Carta," The British Library,
    n.d., http://www.bl.uk/
    collections/treasures/
    magnatranslation.html
    (March 27, 2007).

94 quoted in Danziger and
    Gillingham, 254.

97 Ibid., 253.

99 quoted in Holt, 362.

100 quoted in Danziger and
    Gillingham, 255.

103 Ibid., 257–258.

108 Coke, afterword.

111 Universal Declaration of
    Human Rights, *United
    Nations Website*, n.d., http://
    www.un.org/Overview/rights
    .html (March 27, 2007).

112 Henry of Bratton, *De Legibus
    et Consuetudinibus Angliae*
    (Bracton on the Laws and
    Customs of England), ca.
    1210–1268, in *Harvard Law
    School Library, Bracton
    Online*, April, 2003, http://
    hlsl.law.harvard.edu/bracton/
    Common/SearchPage.htm
    (March 27, 2007).

115 quoted in Holt, 10.

116 Ibid.

116 Ibid.

118 U.S. National Archives and
    Records Administration,
    Declaration of Independence,
    n.d., http://www.archives.gov/
    national-archives-experience/
    charters/declaration.html
    (March 27, 2007).

121 U.S. National Archives and
    Records Administration, *The
    Constitution of the United
    States*, n.d., http://www
    .archives.gov/national-
    archives-experience/charters/
    constitution.html (March
    27, 2007).

122 Rudyard Kipling, "The Reeds
    of Runnymede," *Britannia
    Internet Magazine*, 2007,
    http://www.britannia.com/
    history/kipling.html (March
    27, 2007).

SELECTED BIBLIOGRAPHY

PRIMARY SOURCES

Britannia Internet Magazine. *Sources of British History: The Charter of Liberties of King Henry I*, 1997. http://www.britannia.com/history/docs/charter.html (March 27, 2007).

British Library. "Magna Carta." *British Library*, n.d., http://www.bl.uk/collections/treasures/magnatranslation.html (March 27, 2007).

Roger of Wendover, *Flowers of History*. Translated by J. A. Giles (London: Henry G. Born, 1849). Available online at the Internet Medieval Sourcebook, June 1997, http://www.fordham.edu/halsall/source/wendover1215.html (March 27, 2007).

Shakespeare, William. *The Life and Death of King John*. Edited by W. J. Craig, 1914. Available online at *Bartleby.com*, 2005, http://www.bartleby.com/70/index25.html (March 27, 2007).

SECONDARY SOURCES

Breay, Claire. *Magna Carta: Manuscripts and Myths*. London: British Library, 2002.

Coke, Sir Edward. *Coke on Magna Carta: The Second Part of the Institutes of the Laws of England*. Reproduction of the 1797 ed. Palmdale, CA: Omni Publications, 1998.

Danziger, Danny, and John Gillingham, *1215: The Year of Magna Carta*. New York: Simon & Schuster, 2003.

Holt, J. C. *Magna Carta*. 2nd ed. Cambridge, UK: Cambridge University Press, 1992.

McKechnie, William Sharp. *Magna Carta: A Commentary on the Great Charter of King John*. Glasgow, Scotland: Maclehose, 1914. Available online at Online Library of Liberty. April 20, 2004. http://oll.libertyfund.org/Home3/HTML.php?recordID=0346 (March 27, 2007).

National Archives of England, Wales, and the United Kingdom. "Exhibitions and Treasures, Middle Ages (1066–1484)." *National Archives of England, Wales, and the United Kingdom.* n.d. http://www.nationalarchives.gov.uk/museum/dates.asp?date_id=1 (March 27, 2007).

Poole, A. L. *Domesday Book to Magna Carta, 1087–1216,* 2nd ed. New York: Oxford University Press, 1993.

Reeves, Compton. *Pleasures and Pastimes in Medieval England.* New York: Oxford University Press, 1998.

Robbins Library. "The Robin Hood Project." University of Rochester, n.d., http:www.lib.rochester.edu/camelot/rh/rhhome.stm (March 27, 2007).

Saul, Nigel, ed. *The Oxford Illustrated History of Medieval England.* New York: Oxford University Press, 1997.

FURTHER READING AND WEBSITES

BOOKS

Campbell, Kumari. *United Kingdom in Pictures*. Minneapolis: Twenty-First Century Books, 2004.

Cantor, Norman F. ed. *The Encyclopedia of the Middle Ages*. New York: Viking, 1999.

Dyer, Christopher. *Everyday Life in Medieval England*, 2nd ed. London: Hambledon and London, 2003.

Hamilton, Janice. *The Norman Conquest of England*. Minneapolis: Twenty-First Century Books, 2008.

Keen, Maurice. *The Penguin History of Medieval Europe*. New York: Penguin Books, 1968.

Reynolds, Susan. *Kingdoms and Communities in Western Europe, 900–1300*. 2nd ed. New York: Oxford University Press, 2002.

WEBSITES

"British History"
http://www.britannia.com/history
From timelines to trivia, this site from Britannia Internet Magazine highlights the people, places, and events in the history of Great Britain. The site includes some primary documents.

The Constitution of the United States
http://www.archives.gov/national-archives-experience/charters/constitution.html
View the U.S. Constitution, including the Bill of Rights, at the website of the U.S. National Archives.

Declaration of Independence
http://www.archives.gov/national-archives-experience/charters/declaration.html
The U.S. National Archives website includes the text of the Declaration of Independence and many other important documents.

"Focus on Domesday"
> http://www.learningcurve.gov.uk/FocusOn/Domesday/default.htm
> The National Archives of England, Wales, and the United Kingdom created this online exhibit specifically for students. It includes clear descriptions of the events surrounding the Domesday Book, excerpts from primary documents, and fun facts.

"Magna Carta and Its American Legacy"
> http://www.archives.gov/exhibit_hall/featured_documents/magna_carta/legacy.html
> This online exhibit on the U.S. National Archives and Records Administration explores the influence of the Magna Carta on the founders of the United States.

"Monarchs and Leaders"
> http://www.bbc.co.uk/history/state/monarchs_leaders.
> This page from the British Broadcast Corporation's website features lively articles and illustrations, and traces the lives of the English monarchs, with discussions ranging from their personal traits to their effects on history.

The Official Web Site of the British Monarchy
> http://www.royal.gov.uk/output/Page1/asp.
> Along with information on the present-day monarchy in Great Britain, this website covers the history of the kings and queens of England, with illustrations and links to additional sources.

"The Reeds of Runnymede"
> http://www.britannia.com/history/kipling.html
> Read famous British author Rudyard Kipling's poem about the Magna Carta on the Britannia Internet Magazine website.

United Nations: Universal Declaration of Human Rights.
> http://www.un.org/Overview/rights.html
> Read the United Nations Universal Declaration of Human Rights.

INDEX

Flanders, 73; invades
Normandy, 60–63; and John,
56–57; loses French fleet at
Damme, 69; and Richard I,
50, 52–53

primary source research,
124–125

property and wealth, 8;
management of, 29–30

Ranulf de Blundeville, 76–77

relief, 17, 43, 66, 85–86

religion and church life, 35–39,
121–122. *See also* Innocent
III (pope); Roman Catholic
Church

research methods, 124–125

Revere, Paul, 120

Richard I (king, "Lion Heart"),
50–57, 149

rights of citizens, 6

Robert (Duke of Normandy) 41

Robin Hood, 54–55

Rochester Castle, 98–99,
100–101

Roger of Wendover, 103,
128–129

Roman Catholic Church, 35–39,
70–71, *See also* Innocent III
(pope)

royal forests, 12–13, 49, 90–91

Runnymede, England, 80–81, 93

Scotland, 102

scutage, 16–17, 66, 85–86

Shakespeare, William, 65

sheriffs, 87

Stephen (king), 44–46

tenant system, 20–21, 29

timeline of events, 136–141

town life, 33–35

United Nations, 111

United States: Constitution and
Bill of Rights, 120–121;
Declaration of Independence,
118–119

Universal Declaration of Human
Rights, 111

villeins, 31

wardship, 14–15, 67

"What Say the Reeds at
Runnymede?" (Kipling), 122

William de Braose, 68

William I (king, "William the
Conqueror"), 8–11, 18, 27,
41

William II (king, William
Rufus), 41, 43

ABOUT THE AUTHOR

Before she started writing books for children, Debbie Levy earned a bachelor's degree in government and foreign affairs from the University of Virginia, as well as a law degree and master's degree in world politics from the University of Michigan. She practiced law with a large Washington, D.C., law firm and worked as a newspaper editor. Her previous books include *Rutherford B. Hayes, John Quincy Adams, Lyndon B. Johnson,* and *The Vietnam War.* Levy lives with her husband, two sons, dog, and cat in Maryland.

PHOTO ACKNOWLEDGMENTS